POLAND
A Study in
National
Idealism

a

POLAND

A Study in
National Idealism

BY MONICA
M. GARDNER

Author of
"Adam Mickiewicz"

NOS·NE·CESSES
THOMA·TVERI

BURNS & OATES, LTD.
28 Orchard Street
London W
1915

Printed in England by The Westminster Press,
411a Harrow Road, London, W.

L A race slave n'a pas encore bâti ses cathéd-
rales ni fait ses croisades. La France, dans
l'histoire des croisades, pourrait trouver
la mesure de sa force morale. L'Allemagne doit
étudier sa cathédrale de Cologne, et s'humilier
devant ce monument du passé ; mais la Pologne
n'a qu'à consulter sa tradition vivante, son Ame.

ADAM MICKIEWICZ, *Les Slaves.*

CONTENTS

PREFACE

AT this moment, the eyes of England are once more turned towards Poland. The object for which I have written this book is to give the English reader some faint conception of the idealism and the patriotism by which Poland has preserved her life through more than a hundred years of suffering and oppression. The literature that was born of her sorrows has been, as I have endeavoured to point out in the following pages, one of the chief factors in the maintenance of that life, and almost the only method of self-expression that has been possible to a country, debarred as Poland has been from normal existence. The production of the Polish poets is a splendid form of art : but even more is it a great movement of national aspiration. Hence my book is not so much a study in Poland's literature as an attempt to illustrate the soul of a nation which, were it only for her devoted patriotism and fidelity to her ideals under overwhelming difficulties, should command universal sympathy. For this purpose, I have in the first chapter given a brief account of the condition of Poland since the partitions.

A word must be said as to my mode of dealing with Russia's past treatment of Poland. It is a subject that is necessary to be faced in a work on Poland if any sort of justice is to be done to the

Poles. The Russian nation, now that she has shaken herself free from Prussian influence, has promised to redress the wrongs that Poland has suffered at her hands. The greater these wrongs have been, the more profound will be the admiration of Europe when she beholds their reparation.

It has been impossible in a book of this scope to give more than a sketch of such poets and teachers as Mickiewicz and Krasinski. I have already published a monograph on the former (*Adam Mickiewicz, the National Poet of Poland*, London, 1911), and I have in preparation a study on the life and work of Krasinski.

For the sake of the English reader unacquainted with the Polish language, I have generally translated the Polish Christian names into their English equivalents. As the Polish crossed l is a complicated matter for printers and readers ignorant of Polish, I have—although it is incorrect to do so—replaced it where it occurs by the simple l, according to the custom of many French and English writers on Poland. Certain letters of the Polish alphabet that present special difficulties I have rendered phonetically ; but as it has not been always possible to do this, I have indicated a few rules on the pronunciation of Polish that may be useful to the reader.

Chapters V. and VII. and portions of my first and second chapters have already appeared in the *Quest*. Through the courtesy of the editor, Mr. G. R. S. Mead, I am enabled to reprint them here. With the exception of the chapters on *Anhelli* and Ujejski, the present book has been written after the outbreak of the war. I have therefore been cut off from communication with my friends and correspondents in Poland. But the generous assistance which they gave me in the past and in my work on Krasinski, about which I was able to consult them before the cataclysm swept down upon us, has been of the greatest help to me in what I have been writing during these terrible months, while their country has been devastated by all the horrors of war. I therefore express my deeply grateful thanks to my friend, Mr. Edmund Naganowski, to Dr. Kallenbach, and to Professor Zdziechowski. I am also much indebted to Mr. Ladislas Mickiewicz, the son of Adam Mickiewicz, and to my brother, Dr. Edmund Gardner.

My earnest hope in offering this little book to English readers is that it may arouse their sympathy for the Polish nation.

1915. M. M. G.

Note.—Since the above words were written, the news reached me of the death in Poland of my friend, Edmund Naganowski. With him his country loses one whose labour in her behalf was unceasing. To those who, like myself, were honoured with his friendship, and who found in him the strongest, the most devoted and sympathetic of friends and advisers, his loss can only be a lifelong and irreparable bereavement.

NOTE ON THE PRONUNCIATION OF POLISH

The Polish C—an English ts, but has a softer and somewhat hissing sound when it precedes i, or when it is accented as in ć.

Ch—strongly aspirated h, as in the Scotch loch.

Cz—ch in cherry.

Dz—j, as in jam.

J—y.

Ó—oo as in rood.

Rz—the French j, as in Jean.

Ś, Si—a very soft hissing form of sh.

Sz—sh.

W—v.

Ż, Zi—French j.

The accent in Polish is almost invariably on the penultimate as, Mickie'wicz.

CHAPTER I

THE LAST HUNDRED YEARS

FOR more than a hundred years, Poland has presented to Europe the spectacle of a nation rent asunder. Her nationality has been proscribed and oppressed. The common rights of race possession have been denied to her. She has risen in arms for her liberties, only to be crushed. She has suffered the basest treachery and the bitterest disillusions. Eighty years ago, Montalembert, in a famous phrase, gave her the name of the " nation in mourning." That title has never lost its application.

In 1772 and 1793, the first two partitions of Poland were effected : the first between Austria, Russia and Prussia, the second between Russia and Prussia. After the second partition Kościuszko, arming the peasants with scythes, rose at the head of the nation in a desperate attempt to save the national independence. The armies of Russia and Prussia were too strong for him. He was carried, a wounded prisoner, from the lost field of Maciejowice. Suvorov, the Russian commander, then marched on Warsaw. The city was taken after an appalling massacre of the inhabitants of its suburb, Praga, in which thousands perished by the sword or by fire, or were drowned in the river as they fled, with a broken bridge before them, from Suvorov's soldiers. The cause of Poland was

B

vanquished; and the third partition of Poland between Austria, Russia and Prussia followed in 1795. By this proceeding, a crime almost unparalleled in history, assuredly without a shadow of political or moral justification, Poland as a state ceased to exist.

But the Polish nation never gave up the hope of resurrection. She lived on, as she has lived to the present hour, struggling for her nationality, clinging to it, and preserving it.

After the third partition, what remained of the Polish army enrolled itself under Napoleon's banners. Led by the national flags, commanded by their own officers, the Polish legions shed their blood in torrents for the man who they believed would give them back their country. Napoleon's betrayal of the Polish cause was only one among the many deceived hopes and broken pledges of which the unhappiest of nations has been the victim. The Treaty of Tilsit in 1807 has been called by the Poles the fourth partition of Poland; for, on this occasion, Napoleon did nothing more for those whose loyalty remained with him till his death than to create, under his protection, the Duchy of Warsaw. Ruled by the French laws that Napoleon imposed upon it, its army, with Joseph Poniatowski at its head, was, however, national, and did brilliant service on the side of France. For nine years the little state was swept by the war, till, at last, peace was restored to Europe.

At the congress of Vienna that met in 1815 to readjust the political balance, the question of Poland was one that came prominently forward, as it will do again. The ancient Republic of Poland was not re-established. It was once more divided between the three original partitioning powers. To Austria fell Galicia, with the exception of Cracow. Prussia kept the Duchy of Posen, West Prussia, Thorn, and Danzig. Russia secured the rest of the Duchy of Warsaw, Lithuania, and those eastern provinces of Poland that stand between the Muscovite empire and Western Europe. The express stipulation was made that in each of these three divisions the language, religion, and nationality of the Poles were to be maintained and respected in their entirety. But two further attempts were made to give at least some measure of fuller independence to the Polish nation. Cracow was erected into a tiny stateship under the protection, the irony of which subsequent events fully proved, of Austria, Prussia, and Russia. A part of the Duchy of Warsaw passed, it is true, to Russia ; but under the condition that she should be an autonomous state with the Tsar as her crowned king. Her army, her administration, every branch of her life, were to be Polish and exclusively Polish. And to this day, long after her privileges have been swept away, that part of Poland is spoken of by every Pole as the Kingdom of Poland.

The admirable organization of the newly-founded kingdom proved how rapidly the Poles had learned in the school of adversity. Picked officials filled the posts of trust. The military chiefs, the army, were the soldiers who had been trained by Napoleon. Much was hoped of the Tsar, Alexander I. When an unhappy heir at the court of Catherine II., he had formed a warm friendship with young Adam Czartoryski, son of a princely Polish house, who was retained as a hostage at the same court. In their intimate conversations Alexander promised the Pole that he would restore Poland, and it was through Czartoryski's influence on the Tsar that the Kingdom of Poland owed its foundation. But unfortunately the viceroy whom Alexander chose for the new Polish state was a man of little worth and small patriotism, mistrusted by his fellow-countrymen. The commander-in-chief, appointed likewise by the Tsar, was the latter's brother, the Grand Duke Constantine. This semi-madman, in his transports of mingled insanity and brutality, subjected the proud and high-spirited Polish officers to indignities that drove more than one of them to commit suicide rather than serve under such a leader. In addition to the viceroy and commander-in-chief, a Russian Commissioner was nominated whose office was to play spy upon the Poles. It was this man, Novosiltzov, who brought about the state of things that goaded the Polish nation into the rising of 1830. His spies filled the country. Any careless word resulted in the speaker's arrest. The prisons were filled.

In 1825 Alexander I. died, and was succeeded by his brother, Nicholas I. Two years earlier the famous affair of the Lithuanian student societies took place. Led by the devoted and high-minded Thomas Zan, an association had been formed among the young men at the University of Wilna, under the title of the Philomathians. Their ends were the moral and philanthropic ideals of ardent and generous youths ; patriotic rather than revolutionary. The suspicions of the Russian Government fell upon the society. Its members were imprisoned and many of them put to torture. Numbers were banished to Siberia, while others were exiled to various outposts in Russia. Among the latter was the poet, Adam Mickiewicz, the fast friend of Thomas Zan. He has immortalized the scenes of the imprisonment of himself and the comrades of his youth, most of whom he never saw again, in his drama the *Ancestors*.

These proceedings of Novosiltzov's aroused the resentment of the whole nation. The liberties guaranteed to the Kingdom were now being rapidly trampled underfoot. The country was treated as a conquered province. The situation of the Poles was intolerable ; and on the night of November 29th, 1830, they rose in arms for their treaty rights.

The Rising of 1830 was ill prepared, chiefly by a handful of young men. It was badly organized. There were dissensions among its leaders, lack of discipline. These are its weak points, redeemed by the heroic courage of a people that laid down their lives by thousands rather than see their country perish. The Poles fell, says an eye-witness, like grain before the scythe.* Boys from colleges and schools who, we are told, kept up their studies in the camp in the intervals when they were not fighting, young poets whose songs were sung by the soldiers and who wrote their poems with a baggage waggon for their table, high-born women,

* Quoted by Count Stanislas Tarnowski in *Our History in the Nineteenth Century.* Cracow, 1901 (Polish)

hunters armed with old hunting-guns, peasants with their scythes, seasoned legionaries from the Napoleonic wars, all fought side by side. The Poles held out for ten months against the Russian armies. They won victory after victory. Then came the inevitable hour of defeat by superior forces. At Ostrolenka, where not a Polish gunner but died at his gun, and thousands fell with the national hymn on their lips, the heroism of the Poles was only equalled by their appalling losses. From that hour the Polish arms met nothing but reverses. The Russians marched on Warsaw. In its defence, men and women fought alike. Ordon blew up the fort he was commanding, and Russian and Pole found there a common death. Entrenchments were defended, fought for inch by inch, till not a Pole was left alive. The city could hold out no longer and surrendered, and in September, 1831, the war was ended.

In the interest of historical truth and in justice to the Poles, the sequel of the rising, however painful, must be told in a book that professes to deal with the psychology and the aspirations of the Polish nation. The world is now looking to Nicholas II. to inaugurate a new epoch in the relations between Poland and Russia.

Since the failure of the Rising in 1831, the constitution of the Kingdom of Poland has existed no more except on paper. Her treaty rights were destroyed, her army abolished, her administration taken from her and removed to Petersburg. The universities of Warsaw and Wilna were closed. Schools were shut, and the Russian language enforced on those that still were allowed to remain.

Russian officials took the place of Poles. The libraries and artistic treasures of the nation were transferred to Russia. Confiscations and fines brought Polish families to ruin. Transportation of forty-five thousand families into the Caucasus and other Russian provinces parted husbands and fathers from their homes for ever. Hundreds of innocent persons suffered the penalty of death. The numbers of those who were sent for life to dungeons or to the mines of Siberia are said to exceed computation. Children were torn from the country and carried off by the Cossacks to Russia, never to be seen again.

Yet the strong national spirit lived on in every part of Poland and wherever, in their enforced wanderings over the world, her exiles went. Hopeless attempts at a fresh rising, mainly instigated by young Poles stealing secretly into the country from abroad, continued, always to be discovered and punished with Siberia or death.

Then it was, in the years following the Rising of 1830, that the movement known as the Polish Emigration set in. Those who were banished from Poland, or who escaped death only by flight, or who chose to live beyond the frontier to carry on the work in their nation's behalf that was impossible in the country itself, took refuge in foreign lands, and especially in Paris. Every class was represented; aristocrats like Adam Czartoryski, who had in happier days influenced for good the policy of Alexander I, the friend of his youth, and who had now lost all for Poland; the generals and soldiers of the Rising, artisans, priests, the poets who gave Poland the magnificent literature

that might not be heard within her boundaries.
All degrees of mental and physical wretchedness
were to be found among their ranks. They were
exiled for ever from their country and from those
they loved. Too often they could not learn the
fate of their families or communicate with those
members of them who still remained in Poland.
Most of them were plunged in dire poverty ; all
of them in constant suspense and harrowing
anxiety as to what terrible news, whether personal
or national, the next post from Poland would
bring them. They shared one common certainty :
that they would live to return and see Poland free.
Their death in the foreign city, where their graves
are still piously visited by their fellow Poles, was
the only end to their desire.

I shall deal with the condition of the Poles in
Prussian Poland later in this chapter.

Under Austria the Galician Poles were treated
as the victims of a brutal war rather than as a
nation whose rights had been ratified in a European
congress. The policy of Metternich was to crush
every Polish element underfoot. The stipulations
of the Treaty of Vienna were regarded as non-
existent. The offices of the national government
were filled by Austrians or Czechs. Punishment
by death was inflicted with appalling frequency
on those who held Polish aspirations. The Polish
language was abolished in the schools. It was a
penal offence for the Polish students to be heard
speaking Polish to each other even out of lesson
hours, or to be caught reading in Polish. House
to house inquisitions were made for Polish books.
Those who possessed them, read them or lent

them, went to prison. The publication of Polish writings was attended with almost prohibitive difficulties on account of the heavy censorship. Public works, such as the maintenance of hospitals, roads, and so on, were completely neglected by the Government. The country, ruinously taxed, became poorer day by day.

Here, as to Russian Poland, came emissaries from Paris, urging insurrection. The prisons were filled with those whose implication the Government discovered or only suspected. Matters were ripening for a rising in the three divisions of Poland; when the year 1846 beheld, not the war originally planned, but one of the most lamentable catastrophes in Polish history.

Certain of the Poles in Paris were preparing a rising on democratic lines. Their representatives endeavoured to persuade the Galician peasants to take up arms, and to compel their landowners, even by force if necessary, to join the movement. Following these came certain agitators, wandering from village to village, playing upon the ignorance of the peasantry, instigating them to turn their weapons, not against the oppressors of their country, but against the Polish nobility. These, it is now known, were the agents of the Austrian government. They were but too successful. Duped and deceived, maddened by drink, the peasants rose against the Polish nobles; fired their mansions, and massacred the inhabitants.

In the same year, Cracow lost her last vestige of independence. The first years of her existence as a separate state had been tranquil. Her trade, her schools and University, had flourished. But

in a city where three official residents represented
the three Powers to which the rest of Poland was
subjected, liberty could not last long. When, in
1846, a general Polish rising seemed imminent,
the Austrian army retired from the town, and
the insurgents, believing that all was in readiness,
instituted a government and issued a call to arms.
That rising was abortive ; and, in the autumn of
the year, Austria seized the city which she has
since retained.

The wave of unrest that in 1848 ran through
the countries under Austrian rule brought an
expectation of better things to Poland, that was
not immediately fulfilled. In the general ferment,
on the pretext of a chance quarrel between a few
soldiers and workmen, the Austrian army bom-
barded Cracow, thus adding another chapter to
the chequered history of the city which, the
sepulchre of Poland's kings and of her greatest
dead, may be called the sanctuary of the nation.
It was not till 1861 that Austria reversed her
Polish policy. The first Galician Diet was then
opened, and a species of autonomy was granted,
with the result that Galicia became, and has continued till this day, the centre of Polish national
life.

The Crimean War, upon which the Poles
founded brilliant hopes, had passed, leaving behind it none of the results for which they had
confidently looked. Italy had won her deliverance,
Hungary her constitution. To the Poles it seemed
as if their hour must also be approaching. While
this thought was seething in the hearts of the
Polish youth, events happened in Warsaw that

precipitated the rising of 1863. On the 25th of February, 1861, the Poles were celebrating in a pacific and religious fashion the anniversary of the battle of Grochów, one of the victories in the last rising. Two days later, on February 27th, a similar peaceful demonstration led to a collision between the Russian troops and the people. The soldiers fired upon the unarmed crowd outside the church of the Bernardines, with the result that five Poles were killed. All appeals to the Viceroy were in vain. Then, on April 8th, occurred that terrible scene outside the castle when a crowd of unarmed Polish men and women, who stood there in a silent protestation against their wrongs, were massacred in cold blood by order of Gortchakov.

It had been urged upon the Tsar, Alexander II, that, if a rising were to be averted, the severity with which the nation had been treated since 1831 must be relaxed. The Tsar refused to renew the constitution of the Kingdom; and instead appointed the Pole, Wielopolski, as the minister of religion and education. In some respects, such, for instance, as the improvement of the schools, and the re-opening of the University of Warsaw, Wielopolski did much for the amelioration of the country; but, on the other hand, his desire for conciliation with Russia led him into deplorable acts of injustice that effectually exasperated the Polish youth. The people were on fire with patriotic and mystic fervour. Singing on their knees the national hymn, they were shot down where they knelt, slain in their churches. In 1863 a drastic conscription was levied in order to remove the youths of Poland from the country. Two thousand of them were seized in their beds at night, and despatched to Siberia and the Caucasus. This was the match to the explosion. The young men who were left escaped to the woods and flew to arms.

Doomed from the beginning, the Rising of 1863 was a disastrous attempt. It dragged on for a year in the nature of guerilla war; a struggle in the woods, carried on by small bands of Polish youths, armed with any weapon upon which they could lay their hands. Beaten wherever the Russian regiments and cannon came in force against them, they then reappeared in some other place, frequently victorious over small detachments, fighting on in the certainty that Europe would come to their help. Those who were captured were shot, hung, or sent to Siberia. The farms and dwellings of any person who had sheltered them or given them provisions were burnt to the ground, and the inhabitants killed or imprisoned.

Napoleon III, England, and Austria all addressed their remonstrances to Alexander II. That he could afford to disregard them is owing to the rising influence of Bismarck. The latter entered into a secret understanding with Russia. England, with the threat of the Prussian annexation of Schleswig-Holstein, retired definitely from the championship of Poland. Napoleon's proposal that a congress should be held to ameliorate the condition of the Poles fell to the ground; and henceforth Europe abandoned the Polish nation to her fate. To the policy that then began may be ascribed the disasters that are now ravaging the world.

The penalty that desolated Russian Poland, when the insurrection was at last stamped out, resolved itself into something little short of a war of extermination against every semblance of Polish nationality. We will confine ourselves to such facts of this terrible story as are necessary to tell ; we trust, as a closed chapter.

Henceforth the Kingdom was no longer ruled even by a viceroy who was Russia's nominee, but by a governor-general, and as a conquered district known by the name of the Vistula province. The nation groaned under a bondage to which modern history offers nothing similar. The Poles were sent by thousands, on the merest suspicion, with no attempt at a judicial inquiry, to languish in the mines of Siberia. Women and innocent children were deported there, as convicts, in convict dress. The reign of terror established by Muraviev in Lithuania was such that the Russians refused to touch his hand in friendship on his return to Petersburg ; and it is with the sobriquet of the " Hangman," which his countrymen gave him, that his name has gone down to posterity. Students were expelled from school for speaking their mother tongue in the streets to their schoolfellows. Polish was forbidden in the churches, in every public place, in private talk. In the hospitals, including those devoted to the care of children and foundlings, the sick were not allowed to hear their own language. The University of Warsaw was, and has remained, entirely Russianized. Russian masters were placed in every school.

Even in the village schools the Polish children might only learn in Russian. The childish minds were taught falsification of the two dearest inheritances of a patriotic and devout race—their faith and national history. Bishops were driven from their dioceses, parishes were deprived of priests, and the church of Poland subjected to a systematic oppression that has continued ever since. The Polish landowners were dispossessed of their estates ; Poles forbidden to buy land. Enormous taxation completed their ruin.

With the course of fifty years, the rigour of some of these measures has been abated. Others stand as they were. Others have been added. When, in 1906, the Russian Duma was opened, and the Poles granted representation, to Poland, as to all Russia, it seemed as though a new era of freedom had dawned. Once more this most tragic of nations passed through a bitter disillusion. That the sorrows of Poland will now be a thing of the past is the hope of Europe and the world.

We will now turn to the Polish subjects of Prussia. They have suffered from a rule which, for its drastic brutality, no less than for its galling pettiness, is, say the Poles, more intolerable than any other. We are now unhappily familiar with Pan Prussian methods. It is that machinery which, since the days of Bismarck, has been employed in the vain task of crushing out Polish nationality.

The favourite anti-Polish colonization scheme of the Prussian Government dates from the years following the third partition. From 1799 to 1807 a fund, paid out of the taxes levied on the Poles, and a crown grant were devoted to the purpose of

settling Germans on Polish soil. The Napoleonic
wars diverted the attention of Prussian policy for
a time into other directions, and it appeared as
though Prussia were prepared to respect the rights
of the Poles she governed. But at the time of the
Polish insurrection of 1830 a change set in. Polish
soldiers who had crossed the Russian frontier into
Prussia were handed over by the latter to Russia
and to their death, or shot in cold blood by the
Prussian authorities ; and the Prussian Government began to treat its Polish subjects more
severely than it had hitherto done. When the
Polish rising broke out in 1863, Prussia entered
into agreement with Alexander II. Not only were
those Polish insurgents who had taken refuge in
Prussia imprisoned and sent back into Russia,
but, at the instigation of Bismarck, Prussia under-
took to support Russia in her reprisals against
Poland. Hence the similarity between the measures
of repression adopted by the Russian and Prussian
governments against the Poles in their respective
dominions. During the Franco-Prussian war,
Germany made a bid for Polish support by per-
mitting the military bands to play the Polish airs
as the Poles went to battle, which concession is
now withdrawn. But when she found herself
victorious, she had no further object in conciliat-
ing the Poles. She then, led by Bismarck, proceeded to the persecution which, in flagrant
violation of the Treaty of Vienna and of Frederick
William IV's solemn promise to protect the
liberties of his Polish subjects, has continued to
gather volume till it has reached its present
lengths.

The Kulturkampf that, in the seventies of the nineteenth century, Bismarck directed against the Catholic Church in Germany fell upon Prussian Poland with the double violence of an attack upon religion and nationality. The Archbishop of Gnesen and Posen, Ledochowski, was thrown into prison for refusing to allow the Polish children to be taught their faith in German. He remained two years there, and was then banished. Priests were expelled from their parishes, penalized for administering the sacraments. Over two hundred thousand Polish Catholics were left without a priest to minister to them the consolations of their religion. Convents were closed and religious orders banished, several of which have never been permitted to return. The Kulturkampf died out. Then Bismarck opened his direct war upon the Polish nation.

In 1885 forty thousand Poles, men, women, and children, were ruthlessly deported from Prussian Poland at forty-eight hours notice, because they were Poles who were not Prussian subjects. They were turned out into the world, homeless and friendless, to find a living as best they could. Soon the Government was faced with a serious shortage of labour in consequence of the thousands of Polish labourers it had lost : and it proposed to import Chinese coolies into the heart of Europe to supply the place of the hardworking, frugal Pole who might work no longer in his country.

In the following year—1886—the Colonization Bill was passed. Enormous grants of money went to the foundation of the Commission of

Colonization, by which Polish land is bought up and parcelled out at small rates to German settlers. The Poles parried this attack by founding their own land-bank, by which they in their turn bought up land and let it out to Polish peasants. Again and again immense sums have been voted by the Prussian Government for German colonization of Polish lands ; and yet it was proved that the Poles bought more rapidly than the Germans, and that this attempt at Prussianization was a failure. In 1896, therefore, the Government established its own first right of purchase. From thenceforth no Pole can ever re-acquire land that has passed into the possession of the Commission. The struggle for the soil, between those to whom it has belonged for centuries and the Germans who are determined to drive them out, continuously proceeds. In the centre of the Polish population German colonists are planted, with German schools, Lutheran churches and parsonages, for which the Pole pays by heavy taxation—thus forced to contribute to his own ruin. And yet, as the Pole still continued to gain ground instead of losing it, the German Government went further. A bill of 1907 prohibited Poles from building dwellings even on their own land. The poor Polish peasant, whose dearest dream is to possess some portion of his mother earth as his own, who will toil for that cherished desire during a life-time, thus found himself brought up against the bitter fact that the simple joys for which he had striven so long, the home on his own plot, were snatched away from him just as he had won them. The cases consequent on this law, that occurred shortly before

the outbreak of the present war, illustrate at once
the tragedy and the absurdity of Prussian methods.
A peasant was compelled to sleep in a caravan on
his own field, as he might not build a house. A
miller was driven to dig a cave to shelter himself
and his fourteen children on the river banks. He
might not have any other resting place, nor even
sleep in his mill.

Then came the Expropriation law, passed in
1908, by virtue of which the Polish landowner is,
at the bidding of the government, evicted from
his estate. The year before this measure became
law the great Polish novelist, Henryk Sienkiewicz,
himself a Russian subject, addressed an appeal to
the whole civilized world against the oppression
of which his fellow Poles under the Prussian
Government are the victims. It runs as follows :

" Sir,—The twentieth century has seen an
unheard of act carried out, an insult against
civilization, against right, against justice, and
against all those humanitarian conceptions which
are the foundation of life and of the intellectual
culture of modern society.

" For a long time, a Commission of Colonization
has existed in Prussian Poland, with the object of
buying Poles' estates in order to settle Germans
on them, and which pays for these properties
with funds to which the Poles themselves, Prussian
subjects, have been forced to contribute by taxes.
If to that we add the martyrdom of Polish children
in the German schools and the recently projected
law forbidding the use of the Polish language in
public assemblies, it seems impossible that iniquity

and the contempt of equality before the law could
be pushed further. And yet the Government,
whose principle is that ' might is right,' has not
been content with this.

"In fact, a bill for *compulsory expropriation* has
been presented to the Prussian Diet. The Poles,
who are subjects of the Prussian sceptre, will be
at last driven forth from that soil which is their
native land, that beloved earth where, for centuries, long generations have been born, have
lived, and are buried.

"The part of Poland which the monarchy of
the Hohenzollerns has seized has never lit the
flames of revolution. She bears herself pacifically,
she strictly fulfils the painful duties that events
have imposed upon her. She pays the taxes, and
furnishes a military contingent whose valour
Bismarck himself more than once admired. Thus,
when the first news of this enforced expropriation
appeared in the European press, the project was
universally looked upon as a savage and mad
lucubration of some fanatics bereft not only of
moral sense but of all reason. Men felt sure that
a civilized state, which recognizes the right of
property as the corner stone of the social edifice,
would never go so far as to trample underfoot with
such brutality both that principle itself and the
most elementary conceptions of justice. Nobody
believed such a crime possible in a society that
calls itself Christian and considers itself as
such.

"And yet the Chancellor Bülow has presented
to the Prussian Diet a bill for the *compulsory expropriation of the Poles*, and the Diet, instead of

sending the Chancellor to the study of law and morality, sent on the bill to the Commission.

" The official news of this act has now been spread abroad through all the world; and, to the honour of humanity, it must be stated that everywhere it has called forth a unanimous cry of protestation and indignation. The European press without distinction of side and party—and with it all the independent German press—has condemned the action of the Prussian Government as a shameful attack on the natural rights of humanity and against the Constitution that is in force in the kingdom of Prussia.

" Every government, even the one in question, is obliged to reckon with that universal indignation and that universal contempt.

" But we Poles would wish this protest against barbarism to endure as long as possible, and to take on the vastest proportions. This is why we do not consider the voice of the press sufficient, obliged as it is to be occupied each day with new events. This protest will not obtain durability, and at the same time an immense authority, unless the most eminent representatives of science, literature, and art throughout the whole world consent to express their opinion individually. That would be the final judgment of the universal conscience in the face of a crime that is without precedent; and it would also be the most powerful plea for the defence of an important portion of a civilized nation which has deserved well of humanity.

" There is no question here of interfering with the internal affairs of the Hohenzollern monarchy. The question is a matter on which every civilized man has the right to speak, and, above all, those who are among the nations the pillars of civilization and intellectual culture.

" It is for this reason that, Sir, we address ourselves to you, earnestly begging you to pronounce your opinion upon the bill presented by the Prussian Government, the object of which is to tear their land from the Poles by means of compulsory expropriation. Naturally we do not suppose for a single moment that your opinion can be anything else than a word of indignation and reprobation ; but a public reproach, coming from a man like you, will be the condemnation of the greatest infamy in the history of the twentieth century. Your answer will fill the Polish nation with ardour and with hope, and will also be a powerful support to all upright men in Germany who, unwilling to see their country dishonoured in the eyes of the whole universe, fight steadily against the odious design of the Prussian Government."

The Expropriation Bill was first put into execution in October, 1912, when four Polish landowners were given orders to quit their homes. The so-called compensation that they received was so inadequate that they found their fortunes reduced by one quarter or one third. On the eve of the war a bill was under consideration which, if passed, will disqualify every Pole from holding property in that part of his country that at present belongs to Prussia.

The battle for the Polish language proceeds on equal lines with the struggle for the land.

In 1887 the Polish language was forbidden in the elementary schools, with the exception of the prayers and religious instruction, which remained Polish. In 1905 that exception was withdrawn ; and from that time the Polish child has been compelled to learn its religion and to recite its prayers in German. The children refuse to pray or to be taught their faith in the language which they do not understand, which is forced upon them instead of their own mother tongue. They are punished by detention or flogged ; and the instances of Polish children beaten to death by a brutal Prussian master are unhappily not uncommon. A parent whose boy is in a high fever after such a flogging is fined if he does not send the sick child to the house of detention, to which he is condemned because he would not say his prayers in German. The affair at Wreschen is still fresh in the mind of every Pole. The children refused to recite the prayers in German instead of Polish. They were mercilessly flogged. The parents, hearing their children's screams, ran to the schoolhouse and protested. Several of them—breadwinners of the family—were sent to prison. Their number included a poor woman, the mother of young children, who was expecting her confinement. She was condemned to prison for two years, because, maddened at the sight of her children's sufferings, she had abused the schoolmaster. Fines, loss of employment, are the answers that the parents' protests receive.

Polish ladies, determined that the children of their nation shall not be deprived of their birthright, secretly gather them together and teach them gratuitously the truths of their religion in their own language. When discovered, these ladies are thrown into prison, and treated there as common malefactors.

No word of Polish may be uttered in class, or between the children, in the elementary school. The German master refuses to explain his meaning in the only language that the children know, because it is Polish. He illustrates the German word he is teaching by pictures, by signs, in any way rather than allow the pupils to hear their own tongue spoken.

In the secondary schools Polish is proscribed ; Polish history, Polish subjects are dismissed from the curriculum. But here the language may still be taught as an extra lesson, once or twice a week for three-quarters of an hour, and for two years only. Even this concession, meagre enough when we consider the peculiar difficulty and intricacy of the Polish grammar, is hedged round with vexatious hindrances. The Polish boy in the grammar-schools, however marked his abilities, is debarred from scholarships and the government stipends granted to successful scholars, and for which, of course, his parents are taxed. Bullied and persecuted by his German masters and school-fellows, he leads the life of a dog. He is compelled to sit and listen in indignant silence while, before the whole class, the teacher calumniates his nation, and expends his coarse ridicule on the beautiful Polish language and on all that is Polish. For the crime of having founded a private society among themselves for the study of their literature and history, a band of high-class Polish schoolboys

were some years ago expelled from school, condemned to exclusion from every other school in
Germany, which involved the ruin of any such
career as is open to the Pole, with the added
penalty of three years service as privates in the
Prussian army. Likewise, schoolboys found with
Polish histories and works on Polish literature in
their possession run the same danger of expulsion.

The war upon the Polish language is not con-
fined to the limits of the school. Polish parents
are not permitted to have Polish tutors and
governesses for their children. German officials
are authorized to enter a private house at any
moment to ascertain if the children are being
taught in Polish. The patriotic Polish mother will
not desist from teaching her children in their
native tongue their country's history and traditions ; but she is driven to do so in the shelter
of her bedroom, as the one place in her house
which the German inspector is not allowed
to investigate.

The Polish language is forbidden in public
Polish assemblies. At the ticket office the Pole must
ask for his ticket in German ; and, if he does not
know German, he must bring an interpreter with
him. A Polish waiter speaking Polish in a restaurant
is liable to instant dismissal. The peasant who
requires some remedy in the chemist's shop is not
allowed to ask for it in his own language. The
label *Poison* must not be written in Polish over the
medicine purchased by a Pole. The evidence of
the Pole in the law-courts must go through the
medium of a German interpreter. A poor Polish

man or woman who cannot take his or her oath in a language not their own is sent to prison. The Polish soldier, forced to serve in the German army, may not speak Polish with a brother Pole in uniform. The names of the Polish towns and villages, the Polish streets, are rechristened by some German title, as unrecognizable as senseless to the Polish ear. The Polish infant, after being baptized by the name its parents choose, is entered on the register by the German officials under a German name. Letters addressed in Polish are detained at the post-office until the recipient pays a fine. Telegrams may be sent in any and every language—but not in Polish.

What has been well described as " Pole worrying " extends to every branch of existence, small or great. The diplomatic career, rank in the army above a major's, municipal office, the jury, responsible posts on the railway, are all closed to the Pole, unless he will forswear his nationality. The Polish national tunes may not be played. The Polish colours—red and white—may not be worn or used in public decorations. If a Pole happens to wear a red and white tie, he is fined. Boys laying wreaths on the statue of Adam Mickiewicz in Posen—which statue is only permitted to stand in a sequestered spot behind railings—are fined. Priests who allow grown-up persons to join a school excursion are fined. The Polish miners who work the coalfields in Silesia were, till 1913, paid one-half of the wages received by other miners in Germany, besides being the objects of gross tyranny on the part of the German mineowners. Only a determined strike compelled the German Government to redress their grievances.

The Pole is, in fact, treated as the despised and detested alien in the country that has belonged to him centuries before Prussia rose into existence. When Chancellor of the German Empire, Bülow launched a studied insult against the Polish subjects of William II, comparing their high birth-rate to the propagation of a rabbit warren, rabbits in Germany being regarded as vermin. Prussian officers, hearing fellow-travellers talking to each other in Polish, bid them cease speaking " that dogs' language." The teacher in the elementary school brands the language of the pupils in terms that, in this country, children are neither permitted to employ or hear. It may be said with truth that every day of these latter years has increased the weight of Prussia's iron hand on the Poles within her rule. And yet the Poles have not lost ground. They have gained it. They have stood shoulder to shoulder, presenting a front of mingled strength and spirit, with the result that four million people have proved themselves stronger than a great military autocracy. Every attack of the Prussian Government they have parried with a counter thrust. The German buys out the Poles from their land. The Poles buy out the Germans and divide their estates among Polish tenants. The Government boycotts Polish goods. The Poles retaliate by boycotting German goods. The upper class Poles are debarred from ordinary professions. They overcome their old prejudices, and take to trade with admirable results to their nation. Poles are forbidden to speak Polish in their meetings : so they hold meetings over the frontier in Holland—before the war, of course. So invariably is it the case that in a mixed marriage between a Pole and a German the German becomes Polish, and all the children grow up Poles, that the German Government has forbidden its functionaries to marry Polish wives.

It might have been supposed that while Germany is fighting for her existence she would have relaxed her oppression of the Poles. She has scattered broadcast proclamations and promises that the Poles take at their worth as " scraps of paper." And, in the meantime, her treatment of her Poles at home continues on its old lines : so that the Polish deputies have boldly refused to vote the war subsidies. One instance may be recorded here. The Poles in Prussian Poland organized a relief fund for the assistance of their starving and destitute brother Poles in those parts of Poland over which the war has swept. That fund has been confiscated and its originators punished by the Prussian Government.

Abroad, the Polish cities that have fallen into the hands of the German soldiers have all alike suffered from the brutality of Prussian warfare. Czenstochowa has been the scene of unnamable outrages. Kalisz has been destroyed, its women and children deliberately butchered. Warsaw groans beneath the tyranny of the conqueror, who has introduced there the same methods that the citizens of Posen know too well.

Between the Pole and Prussian there is no single bond of sympathy, similarity, or union. Polish idealism, the Polish soul, the Polish tradition, are all at absolute antagonism with the principles of the Bernhardis and Bismarcks and their disciples. And yet—greatest of all the tragedies of this war !—Polish youths, placed by their German rulers in the post of danger, the vanguard, are forced to fight in defence of a cause that is abhorrent to them, and whose triumph would ensure the ruin of their beloved nation. Commanded, in the beginning of the war, to fire upon the Belgians, who were struggling to defend their homes and country, the Polish soldiers, rather than obey the order, shot wide. That Polish boy may be taken as typical who, as the Germans advanced upon Louvain, ran to the hall of the University, tore down the Polish flag and carried it under his clothes on his flight to France, delivered from Prussian capture.

Such is the rough outline of the last hundred years of Poland's history.

Through unparalleled misfortune, against odds under which a less vivid and less heroic people must have gone down, the Polish nation, battling for dear life, has preserved an intense national existence, has kept her ideals unimpaired. Her soul remains, not merely alive, but passionate and invincible. She represents a great principle. She has proved, against fact, that the idea can prevail over brute force ; that the hope, the spiritual conscience of a race, shall save her. Her language, the noblest of Slavonic tongues, lives on the lips of twenty-two million men and women. Her literature, one of the most powerful means by which patriotism and confidence were kept alive in the hearts of an oppressed nation, stands among the magnificent expressions of art and idealism in European history. Beset within and without, exposed to all the deadly moral perils of the conquered and persecuted, she has emerged triumphant from her long ordeal. We may confine ourselves here to one testimony alone, that of a political study published in 1913 by a Polish writer who, far from pronouncing a panegyric upon his nation, does not hesitate to point out her faults with unsparing frankness ; faults, which, as he says :

" Have been redeemed and compensated by . . . nobility of sentiment, chivalrous spirit, uprightness, love of liberty, patriotism, respect for traditions, tolerance, faith in the future, all virtues, which, after our disasters, have preserved us from destruction, and which were like a cuirass against which the arms of our enemies lost the edge. They have not prevented our blood from flowing, but they have saved us from hatred.

" Sweetness and nobility of character, while rendering the work of enfranchisement more difficult, have permitted the Poles to resist the evil influences of servitude, and have guaranteed them against demoralization and degradation. That degradation, that servility, that hypocrisy, that contempt of right, that hatred, those vices of all sorts that are the fruit of oppression, Poland, sweet and noble Poland, has not known them."*

The same writer has stated that the political

* E. Starczewski, *L'Europe et la Pologne.* Paris, 1913.

decadence of Poland which, in part, contributed towards her fall may be traced back to the excessive ease with which the nation expanded. Her conquest of Lithuania and Ruthenia was bloodless. It was without effort that she became the leading power of Eastern Europe. The exact reverse has been her record since her partition. It is by unending sacrifice and struggle that she will have purchased her resurrection. Every great national stake, every detail of homely life with its perpetual background of large issues behind it, from the general principle that Poland must and shall rise again to the incident of a child in Prussian Poland refusing to lisp her prayers in German instead of in the tongue learnt at her mother's knee, has been wrestled for with the heart's blood of a nation. An immense spiritual and mental strength must lie behind such a combat. This strong and set purpose gives the clue to the whole of Polish history, Polish thought, Polish art, since the dismemberment of Poland. Kościuszko, that noblest of national heroes, fought for it. The Polish legions, to their war-cry " Poland hath not perished," fought for it. The youth of Poland, in their two hopeless risings, died for it. It is this that has enabled the Poles in Prussian Poland to stand out, undismayed and unyielding, against the forces of a great military empire. It has inspired the literature of Poland that is its mouthpiece and its messenger. It glows from Matejko's great canvases of Polish history. It speaks through Grottger's pictures of a nation's suffering, through the symbolism of Polish contemporary painters. The mingled fire and sadness of Chopin is but the voicing of the sorrows, the hopes, the heroic memories of his mother country.

While these words are written, Poland is the battlefield of Eastern Europe. Her fields are laid waste, her towns, her villages, her dwellings, are in flames and ruin. Her sons, compelled to serve under one or another of the three powers that partitioned their nation, are forced to fight, brother against brother, friend against friend, to lay down their lives by thousands without the consolation of dying for their country. Devastated by a war in which her all is at stake and in which she has no voice, the condition of Poland is the most tragic in all Europe.

" Three days later," wrote in 1846 the poet Zygmunt Krasinski to a fellow Pole, " the resurrection shall come ; but during those days how many hearts shall break." *

---

* *Letters of Zygmunt Krasinski.* Vol. I, Lwów, 1882. To Constantine Gaszynski, March 30, 1846 (Polish).

CHAPTER II

THE NATIONAL LITERATURE OF POLAND

AFTER the Rising of 1830, the story of Poland becomes that of the long agony of an idealistic and profoundly patriotic race, and of its protracted battle for existence. On one side, in the country itself, the prisons and the mines were the price the Pole paid for remaining a Pole. On the other, beyond the frontiers, there were the throngs of Polish exiles, dragging out lives of poverty, homesickness, and grief. The nation lived on ; but her life was mutilated, abnormal, unlivable.

And yet those years when Poland had no history except a monotony of suffering, no life except that life jealously preserved against proscription and penalty in the heart of every Pole, coincided with the splendid outburst of Polish literature. Unlike the three great empires of the world, Rome, Spain, and England, whose prosperity inspired their golden age of letters, it was the sorrows of Poland that gave birth to her great romantic song which, for its tragic power, its idealism, no less than its haunting beauty, ranks among the noblest productions of European art.

Great as is the literature of Poland from an artistic point of view, it stands on another plane than that of literary value alone. In the first half of the nineteenth century, the Polish poets rose as the national teachers and moral leaders. They spoke to the people held in bondage by the bitterest facts of life, of the hope that would save them. The youths of Poland were prohibited from learning their nation's history, her spirit, her aims in the ordinary channels. They learnt them, therefore, of the poets who taught them the lessons of devotion and self-immolation for a native country ; whose writings kept alive the fires of patriotism, the Polish ideality and moral health, in young souls beset by peril. The national literature was no mere art, an element disconnected with the deep things of life, written for recreation or relaxation. It spoke straight to a stern purpose. It was a weapon, and as powerful a weapon as any that she could have chosen, in the cause of Poland. In this light the Polish poets regarded the poetry they gave their people. The literature they brought forth is, said Mickiewicz, speaking in the Collège de France, " above all things true. Each work is at the same time an action." * Poland's poets were more than her poets. They were her patriots.

The Pole in Poland might not read the masterpieces of his native literature in normal ways. These works were banned by the censor. They were published abroad, often at no little risk to the author. Colporteurs smuggled them into the country. Boys read them behind barred doors, with one of their number posted in the street to give the alarm should the police be near. After one hurried but intense perusal they were thrown

* Adam Mickiewicz, *Les Slaves.*

D

into the fire. Prison and Siberia were the lot of those readers who were discovered. The possession of Mickiewicz's *Ancestors* sent a boy of seventeen to the dungeon, where, maddened with terror lest under the knout he should betray the names of his companions, he burnt himself to death. Hundreds of young men went to Siberia for having read Krasinski's *Temptation*. Often the only means by which the Polish poet could speak to his nation, with any degree of safety to himself or to the reader, was under the protection of an allegory or some sort of veiled meaning, where the Pole could read between the lines. Mickiewicz, in the heart of Russia, wrote an epic of the revenge of the Lithuanian, Konrad Wallenrod, on the Teutonic knights, the oppressors of his country. Every Pole knew for whom the Teutonic knights stood. Krasinski bade his compatriots abjure the weapons of vengeance, and work by love alone; but he did so under the figure of a Greek in the Rome of Heliogabalus. He warned the Polish women against marriage with the enemies of their nation; and the language of his *Summer's Night* is so obscure as almost to fail in its aim. He sought to arm the Polish youth against those seductions of the Imperial Court that had laid their siege to his own soul in vain; yet the elaboration with which he designedly disguised his point could not avert the consequences to his readers. Even in a poem as objective as Slowacki's *Father of the Plague-stricken*, the lamentation of the father over his children dying in the desert is said to represent the desolation of a bereaved country.

Poland, then, was assailed from every side. In anguish of mind her poets and her thinkers sought for some explanation of her tragedy to justify the working of Providence, to save their country from the atrophy and despair that would destroy her as certainly as all exterior persecution. So arose the dreams of a Polish national mysticism, known by the name of Messianism. Its strange and mournful glory casts over Poland's poetry, in the days of Mickiewicz and Krasinski, a faint spiritual kinship with the prophecies of those who saw Sion irradiated with a mystical splendour as the adored of the nations. Poland, says Messianism, was rent asunder that her destruction might bring salvation to the human race. Out of the mysteries of pain and death are born new life and resurrection. Death is the condition of resurrection. The Saviour of mankind redeemed us by embracing death, and after three days in the grave rose again. So, in the political world, one nation has been signalled out to lay down her life. Her sufferings are the price by which the new and better epoch of humanity shall come about. She will rise gloriously to be the spiritual leader of that world, where all nations and governments will be united in Christ and rule in the spirit of Christ. Violence against that spirit of Christ was committed when so hideous a crime against man's rights as the blotting out of a free nation from the land of the living was perpetrated. The restoration of that nation will therefore logically be a return to the ideals of Christ, the first step to their realisation. Various of the Messianists looked to that future period as the third epoch, the reign of the Holy Ghost, thus presenting a curious link with the tenets of Joachim of Flora.

Pushed to its extreme limits, the doctrines of Polish Messianism tended to an exaggeration and a falsity of outlook that were likely to prove injurious to those for whose welfare they were intended. But in its best form, propagated by such a teacher as Krasinski, who made its promises conditional on each individual's purity of soul, it may be taken as a sublime spiritualization of national suffering. The workings of Providence were made clear. The dignity of a great calling was conferred upon a downtrodden people. The Poles were given an end for which to strive. The light of hope was shed over the dark places of grief.

" You all know, my brothers, that we were born in the womb of death," says Krasinski in his prose preface to *Dawn*. " Hence the eternal pain that gnaws your hearts ; hence the incertitude that has become your life. But every end contains already in itself the successive beginning ; the day of death but precedes the hour of wakening. Look closely, and the signs of death will suddenly change for you into the signs of resurrection. Our death was necessary ; necessary will be our resurrection ; and the Word of the Son of Man, the eternal word of life, shall be shed through the social circumference of the world. By our very nationality crucified on the cross of history will be manifested to the conscience of the human spirit that the political sphere must be changed into a religious sphere. The Lord in the whole political sphere, where hitherto He was absent, will be present ; and the vessel of His providence to this end will be no other than the Polish nation."

" One of the two—either the blessed future of humanity is forfeited, or the condition of its fulfilment is the life of Poland."

This idea of the chosen race is the keynote of the great Messianistic poetry of Poland. As in the Hebrew prophets, Jerusalem is the mystic city, the object alike of patriotic and spiritual passion : so the prophet poets of Poland looked towards their country, not solely as the earthly home for which they pined with the human longing of the exile, but as the transfigured heavenly mistress of the soul. Poland is the instrument of God's future favours. She is set apart, therefore, and consecrated. Thus we have Mickiewicz drawing up a manual of religious guidance for those whom he regarded as the apostles of the new civilization. His *Books of the Polish Pilgrimage*, with their curious blending of Biblical flavour, almost homely detail, and the yearning of a man whose face was set to a Jerusalem on a far-off horizon, were addressed to exiles to whom he would not suffer the name of exile to be given. For he would have men know by their demeanour that they were pilgrims in whose hands lay the future of a hallowed country and a new race. Thus we have Krasinski apostrophizing Poland as " The holy one," " Holy Poland." She is no longer to him merely a native land. She is his faith, his idea (*Dawn*). He will liken, to mark the great capital difference, his nation to but one other : Jerusalem, who fell because she spurned

the love that would have saved her (*Psalm of
Good Will*). "The Jerusalem of our return for
which we sigh," is the language in which Mickiewicz expresses to a friend the weariness of his
banishment. "O God of Israel," prays Severyn
Goszczynski; "Thou Who for forty years led
him by the way of victories and pain, through
pathless deserts to the promised land, behold
to-day Israel of the new covenant, the Polish
nation, travels to her promised land. Forsake her
not, O Lord, strengthen her with Thy grace.
Still lead her, as till now Thou ledst her by Thy
girdle till, fed by the blessed word of life Thou
gavest her, she, in the strength of youth, fulfils
her road. And lo! this year may be the year of
her espousals. And I, who lift these prayers to
Thee to-day, pray if only for one moment I may
be at my people's bridal feast" (*The Prayer of a
Poet*). And the poet who watched the fires of the
incendiary blacken his native Galicia placed the
expression of his grief on the lips of a Jeremias,
lamenting over the desolation of the chosen city
(Kornel Ujejski, *The Complaints of Jeremias*).

The poetic symbolization of Poland takes
differing guises. She is the mother, weeping for
her sons. She is the great heavenly archangel of
Krasinski's vision, crowned with the purple of
her sorrows, whose eyes are of the eternal blue,
whose brow flashes with the lightning of God,
before whom the future new-born ages to whom
her suffering has given their being cast down their
wreaths in homage. She is—again and again—
the beloved dead, sleeping in a grave from which
she will rise again. The last word of Messianism

confers on her the lineaments of a Christ of
the nations, dying on the cross of expiation for
the sins of humanity (Mickiewicz, *The Ancestors*,
Part III.) A less usual conception is Bohdan
Zaleski's repentant Magdalen (*The Spirit of the
Steppe*). But behind all these types there is always
the same figure of one beautiful and haloed by
grief ; inexpressibly dear to the heart of him who
wrote ; the one who, in Krasinski's dreams, calls
him, " and I went forth and I go, I know not
where, but that voice I will follow if needs be
even to the end of the world " (*The Dream of
Cezara*). If on one hand Poland is the ethereal,
star-encircled image of a mystic's desire, yet she
is at the same time the living love, spoken of in
the passionate and endearing tones of human
affection.

It is scarcely necessary to insist upon the
patriotic character of the nineteenth century
Polish literature. Devotion to a native country
is one of the most strongly marked features of the
Polish nature. Moreover, the lives of Poland's
poets were, at the time of which we are speaking,
linked with the national cause in an exceptional
manner, difficult of realization by those whose lot
is cast in a land where tradition is the patriotism
of freedom. There was not one of the poets in
the great period of Polish literature whose daily
existence was not ravaged with the personal
afflictions that the public tragedy had brought
upon them. They were nearly without exception
living in exile, penury, loneliness, suspense.
Grinding poverty, domestic trouble, grief at his
absence from his Lithuanian forests, whitened

Mickiewicz's hair before his time. Slowacki, parted for ever from an adored mother, wandered from country to country, beholding in the ruins of Greece the likeness of another land, his heart wrung as he watched the sun set over the Mediterranean by the sadness and the homesickness of the Pole (*The Grave of Agamemnon. Hymn*). The one craving of Bohdan Zaleski, the poet of the Ukraine, was that he might see again the steppes that had nursed his childhood, if but to breathe his last there ; and he died far away from them after half a century of exile. Gaszynski's prayers met his mother's in their mutual loneliness on the Christmas Eve which they could spend together no more (Constantine Gaszynski, *To my Mother on Christmas Eve*). He lived to hear of her murder by Russian soldiers at her door. From his nineteenth year till his death at the age of forty-seven, Krasinski bore a tragedy bitterer than exile, on which his lips were sealed. The heart-sickness of the wanderer, pining to return, runs in mournful undertones through the poetry of Poland, especially in that of Mickiewicz and Bohdan Zaleski ; but it is a larger grief than individual deprivation that gives its tragic accents to Polish literature. Poland's national poetry must of necessity be profoundly sad. " I and my country are one," says Mickiewicz in the *Ancestors*. " My name is Million, because I love millions and for millions suffer torment. I look on my unhappy land as a son upon his father broken on the wheel. I feel the sufferings of the whole nation, as the mother feels within her bosom the sufferings of her child." Or again, the charge laid upon Irydion, the symbolization of Krasinski's national thought, is : "Thou shalt see thy love transpierced, dying ; and the sorrows of thousands shall be born in thy one heart." These words of Poland's two greatest poets may be taken as typical of the vocation and the attitude of the leaders of her literature. There is here no room for egoism. The affliction of their country was to her poets as their own, more than their own. Their poetry is written in the tears of their nation. It is the cry of an inconsolable distress, of a pain personal and intimate as that of a son mourning for the dearest of mothers, a lover for the beloved of his heart.

And yet, whatever its deep melancholy, there is in Poland's patriotic and prophetic song neither pessimism nor despair. Its hope is as eternal as its grief ; victorious over circumstance, however adverse. The idealism, the immense vitality of the Polish race by which it has preserved its life, speak through the literature that is the direct outcome of national calamity, whose themes are built upon a nation's tragedy. Nor is this hope like that figure familiar in English art of one clinging to the last string of a broken lyre. It is rather a radiant certainty, unjustified by a single outward token, rising unshaken in the midst of disaster and defeat, glowing with the mysticism which is the inheritance of the Pole.

" On the third day," writes Mickiewicz when the downfall of the Rising was scarcely a year old, " the soul will return to the body, and the nation will rise from the dead and will free all the nations of Europe from slavery. And two days have already passed : one day passed with the first taking of

Warsaw,* and the second day passed with the
second taking of Warsaw,† and the third day will
arrive, but will not pass away. And as with the
resurrection of Christ sacrifices of blood ceased
on the whole earth, so with the resurrection of
the Polish nation wars will cease in Christendom " (*Book of the Polish Nation*).

"But the day will rise—the day of victory
rises," sang Bohdan Zaleski, as he wandered over
the Roman Campagna, with his heart in the
steppes of the Ukraine. "Oh, to our grand-
children our sorrows shall be told as fables. Christ
is already in our homes. Our youths, living and
strong, new reapers for the harvest, gather
strength by prayer. Blessed are they who believe.
The Lord God, a father in His bounty, visits
more mercifully those whom He orphans. For
them He will fulfil the promise of the Lamb. He
will shake free the earth from its pale, shadowed
husk till it grows green for them, it flowers, it is
the spring. The emissaries from over seas, the
birds of joy, shall make our fields rejoice with
their compelling song. And the heroic, mighty
nation's heart shall inspire the new poet of a
generation new. The burden of his song shall be :
Faith, Hope, and Love. And holy as the sowing
time, so shall the harvest be fruitful, for Poland
reigning queen o'er the Slavonic lands." (*Walk
beyond Rome*).

And this resurrection, so dear to the hearts of
the national poets, did not depend merely or
even mainly on outward events. Naturally they,
as every son of Poland has always done, watched

---

* By Suvorov after the second partition.   † In 1831.

each political event in Europe, either with hope or in the anguish of disillusion, for what it would bring upon their nation. But to the great Polish idealists of the nineteenth century the salvation of their country lay behind what is visible to the eye. Mickiewicz's *Book of the Polish Pilgrimage* is a rule of life given to his fellow Polish exiles ; and in that work there is no hint that Poland shall be restored by the prepotency of earthly powers. Rather her mission and her resurrection depend on the fidelity of the Poles themselves to saving principles. The peculiar spirituality of Krasinski's teaching we shall consider in a later chapter. Three generations have passed since the great prophetical poetry of Poland closed with Krasinski's *Resurrecturis*. Yet Mickiewicz's *Book of the Pilgrimage* was, as recently as the late Russo-Japanese war, found on the bodies of the Polish soldiers, as they lay dead on the battlefields in a cause that was not theirs. There are not wanting countrymen of Krasinski's living now who speak of the day when they first read his work as the moral crisis of their lives, who confess that it was upon his tenets that they henceforth built the edifice of their souls, and that in them they found their defence against the temptations of surrounding evil influences.* A modern political writer appeals to the conclusion of Krasinski's *Irydion* as the basis for an oppressed nation's conduct.†

To this day, the poetry of Mickiewicz, Krasinski, and the band of poets at whose head they stand, is the ethical armoury of Poland, the

---

* M. Zdziechowski, *Vision of Krasinski.* Cracow (Polish).
† E. Starczewski, *L'Europe et la Pologne.* Paris, 1913.

influence that is of paramount consideration in any study of the mental attitude, whether past or present, of the Polish nation. The Poles have seen their country spoliated and desolate, themselves the victims of overwhelming armies and crushing laws. But their poets point steadily to the truth that the idea will prevail against the machinery of war or of autocracy. Resurrection by spiritual strength, response to a high mission, the ultimate triumph of moral over material preponderance, is the inheritance that the poet-patriots left to their people. Or rather, we will not give the name of inheritance to what speaks so directly to the innermost temper and consciousness of the nation that it is indeed part and parcel of the Polish soul. We might more correctly say that the voice of the poets fortified what was already there, raising it to a magnificent expression which remains the truest index to the Polish spirit and mind.

CHAPTER III

THE POET OF A NATION'S SUFFERING:
ADAM MICKIEWICZ

THE genius of Adam Mickiewicz has raised him above all other Polish poets. His fame has travelled the furthest beyond his native land. But it is not merely as the chief glory of their literature that his compatriots honour him with an affection and veneration undimmed by time. He lives in the national history as the man who devoted all his life—a life sad as the annals of his country—to the cause of Poland. The beauty of his moral character and the charm of his personality have endeared him almost as one alive and beloved to the generations which have come after him.

Adam Mickiewicz was born in Lithuania in 1798. He lived the simple life of a wild and remote countryside, where patriarchal customs and ancient traditions still prevailed. As a boy he wandered in forests, as old as time, whose remoter recesses have never to this day been trodden by human foot; about the marshes listening to the cries of the geese and wild birds, gathering the folk-lore of the peasants and the fishermen. When a lad of fourteen, he witnessed the transports of patriotic hope with which all Poland hailed in 1812 the march of Napoleon to Russia. He saw the return of the Grand Army, shattered, fugitive, starving. All these things gave his future poetry their strong distinctive colour.

From a home whose atmosphere was that of simple and homely virtue, domestic affection and ardent patriotism, Mickiewicz passed on to the University of Wilna. Here it was that he began the work for the young men of his country that led him to imprisonment and exile, and from which he may be said never to have desisted. Together with his friend, Thomas Zan, he founded the famous student societies of the Philomathians for the moral improvement of the Lithuanian young men. For them, after he had left the university and become a schoolmaster at Kowno, he wrote his first great poem, the *Ode to Youth*. With a young and generous scorn of egotism—he was but twenty-two when he wrote it—he cries to his comrades :

" Without heart, without soul, those are the nations of skeletons. Oh, youth, give me wings ! Let me soar above a dead world to the heavenly home of enchantment, where enthusiasm works miracles, strews flowers fresh and new, and clothes hope in golden pictures.

" Oh, youth ! Soar thou beyond the horizon's bounds. Gaze down ! There, where eternal night darkens the mighty plain submerged in the chaos of sloth, there is the earth. See how on its stagnant waters rises a reptile in its shell ; rudder and ship and pilot to itself, feeding upon the smaller reptiles' lives. It rises, then it sinks into the deep. To it the wave clings not, it clings not to the wave. And then it bursts against the fragment of a rock.

None knew it when alive, or knows its death. It is the egotist.

" Oh, youth ! The nectar of life is only sweet when it is shared with others. Heaven's joys inebriate our hearts when they are bound together by one golden thread.

" Together, youthful friends ! The happiness of each one is the aim of all, mighty in union, in enthusiasm standing steady. Together, youthful friends ! And happy is he who, fallen in the midst of his career, makes of his dead body a rung of the ladder for others to attain the garden of glory. Together, youthful friends ! Although the road be slippery and steep, and violence and weakness defend the entrance, let violence hurl violence back, and let us learn to conquer weakness in our youth.

" He who a child in the cradle smote off the Hydra's head, in youth shall slay the Centaurs, shall tear its victim out of hell and ascend to heaven on laurels. Reach where the eye does not reach. Break what the reason will not break. Oh, youth ! thy flight shall be as the strength of eagles, as a thunder-bolt thine arm.

" Then shoulder to shoulder ! Let us engirdle the little circle of the earth with the chains that bind us to each other. To one end let aim our thoughts, and to one end let aim our souls. Leave thy foundations far, thou earthy world ! We will force on thee new paths till, shaking off thy rotten skin, thou shalt remember thy past verdant years.

" And as in the lands of chaos and of night, of elements at war, at one ' Let it be,' spoken from the power of God, the living world stood forth, the winds roared, the deep seas flowed, and stars lit up the blue of heaven.

" So in the country of humanity there is still deep night. The elements, men's passions, are still at war. Lo, love shall breathe forth fire. From chaos shall the spiritual world come forth. Youth shall conceive it in its womb, and friendship bind it in eternal bonds.

" The insensate ices and the dark prejudice that hid the light are burst. Hail, dawn of liberty, behind thee is the redeeming sun."

The appeal to unity that may be found in these lines is the poet's protest against the want of harmony that had been politically fatal to his country.* It is said that the *Ode to Youth* acted as a call of the trumpet to the youth of Poland when they rose in 1830.

From the time he wrote the *Ode to Youth*, Mickiewicz continued in the then new road of romantic poetry. He wrote ballads, the earlier part of the *Ancestors*, and the epic *Grażyna*. All these were founded on national themes. The ballads took life from Lithuanian legend. The *Ancestors* has as its setting the half pagan and very ancient Lithuanian feast of the dead, against which Mickiewicz places his hopeless love for Maryla Wereszczak. I shall return to this play. In *Grażyna*, Mickiewicz tells the tale of the princess who, rather than submit to a disgraceful peace with the national enemy, dons her husband's armour and leads the Lithuanians to battle. This again played its part in the Rising of 1830, for under its inspiration the girl heroine of the war,

* J. Kallenbach, *Adam Mickiewicz*. Cracow, 1897 (Polish).

Emilia Plater, fought and died as a soldier in its ranks.

These were the productions of Mickiewicz's early youth. What he next wrote came after he had passed through the ordeal first of imprisonment, then of parting for life from his friends and country. Novosiltzov's persecution of the student societies swept Zan and Mickiewicz, with their associates, into prison. The two former were arrested on October 23rd, 1823. For six months Mickiewicz and his comrades were incarcerated in Wilna. Years afterwards, the poet described the scenes of his prison, with the power alike of genius and of fidelity to the actual events, in the third part of the *Ancestors :* scenes which had branded themselves indelibly on his mind. The brotherhood stood firm, through floggings that to some of their number resulted in death, through solitary confinement in rank dungeons, through the infliction of foul air and putrid food, through the mental torture of harassing judicial inquisitions where any word might send the speaker or his friends to their end. Boys, many of them mere children, were transported in chains to the mines : others condemned to serve in the ranks of the Russian army; exiled, like Zan, to Siberia or to Russia. Mickiewicz himself, after waiting six months in Wilna when released from prison, was banished in the first instance to Petersburg.

In 1824 he left the country which he never saw again, for which he pined with a homesickness that thirty years of poverty and sorrow could not quench. For the following five years he lived in Petersburg, Moscow, and Odessa. His life was

E

more or less that of a prisoner at large, watched by Russian spies, dependent on the pleasure of the police. Wherever he went, he gained the hearts of all who knew him. Much as he detested the system of the Russian autocracy, his soul was too great and his nature too sweet to harbour any rancour against a Russian as such. He was bound by ties of intimate friendship with many a Russian, and especially with the Liberals and poets. In future years, from the land of his freedom he sent them words of mournful remembrance, a farewell to those who had perished for their ideals, an impassioned rebuke to others who had abandoned them (*To my Russian Friends*).

The galling conditions of his life in Russia could not stifle his poetic genius, fretted though it was by its bondage. The *Crimean Sonnets*, *Farys*, which is a wild, glad cry of the desert, *Konrad Wallenrod*, which latter placed Mickiewicz among the great poets of Europe, were all written at this time.

The *Crimean Sonnets* have for their motive a journey that the poet took with the Government's permission in the Crimea. Grief for a lost country throws the shadow of sorrow even over these delicate and exquisite vignettes of a southern, semi-Oriental landscape, painted with the intimate knowledge and love of nature that is such a charming feature in Mickiewicz's poetry. He is in the steppes :

" Already the night falls fast. There is nowhere a road or a knoll. I look to the skies and seek for a guiding star. There, far off, glitters a cloud, there rises the star of dawn. There the Dniester glitters.

There the lights of Akerman shine. Halt! Ah, how still! I hear the flight of the cranes which even the eyes of the hawk reach not. I hear where the butterfly rocks in the grass; where the snake, with its slippery breast, lightly brushes a plant."

And through that silence it is for a voice from Lithuania that he strains his ear (*The Steppes of Akerman*). Among the nightingales, his heart turns to his native forests and marshes (*The Pilgrim*). He stands by the grave of a Polish lady, dead in Tartar slavery, and the stars that shine above it point the road to Poland, whither she gazed, as he gazes, in fruitless yearning. (*Potocka's Grave*).

But the epic *Konrad Wallenrod* ranks above all else that Mickiewicz wrote in Russia, not only as a literary achievement, but still more by reason of its moral significance that gave to Polish psychology the new word of *Wallenrodism*. Mickiewicz published this poem into which he put an exile's sorrow, the dumb rage of a Samson, in 1828. What he could not say openly where discovery stood for Siberia, he said under a tale of the struggle between Lithuania and the Teutonic Knights.

The poem has the strong romantic flavour that with Byron and Scott had come into vogue in Mickiewicz's youth. Minstrels, monks, ladies in towers, are the *dramatis personae*. Konrad Wallenrod is one of the military monks. No one knows his origin. He has but one confidant in the monk, Halban. No smile is ever seen on his lips. Some gloomy mystery envelops him. His prowess in battle and in the lists raise him to the Grand Mastership; but instead of carrying war into

Lithuania he remains passive, allowing the Lithuanians to wreak their will upon the territories of the Order. A feast is held by the Knights. A minstrel enters—in reality, Halban, disguised. He sings of a Lithuanian boy whom the Knights took captive and brought up in their fortress; who, escaping to his natal country, gave up for her sake all that he loved, to return and work revenge upon her enemies by stealth. This is, of course, Konrad's own history, and the mystery is explained. He has schemed to gain the Grand Mastership for patriotic ends, and will use it to serve Lithuania.

The song of the minstrel has a peculiar pathos. We realize that it is Mickiewicz's lament for his exile and for many a Polish boy who would never more see his home.

The Lithuanian child—Konrad—is carried off from his father's house by the Knights. He thus tells his story when in his manhood he has regained his freedom.

" I know not my race or my name, for, as a child, I was taken by the Germans into slavery. Once in the night a loud clamour woke us from slumber. A dawn of fire flashed in the windows. The window-panes crashed, clouds of smoke burst through the building. We ran to the gate. Flames wreathed through the streets, sparks scattered like hail. A terrible cry rang out : 'To arms ! The Germans are in the town. To arms !' My father rushed out with a weapon, rushed out and returned no more. The Germans fell on my home. One carried me off. He tore me away on his horse. I know not what happened next. Only I long, long heard the shriek of my mother. In the midst of the clashing of arms, the crash of the houses that fell, that shriek followed me long, that shriek rang in my ears. Even now when I see a fire, even now when I hear a cry, that shriek still wakes in my soul. This is all that from Lithuania, that from my parents, I carried away. Sometimes I see in my dreams when I sleep the dear forms of my mother, my father, my brothers ; but ever further away, a mist ever darker, ever denser, has hidden their features. The years of my childhood passed on. As a German I lived among Germans. The name they gave me was German. My Lithuanian soul remained. My grief for my family, my hatred for the aliens, remained.

" Among the Germans there was a Lithuanian minstrel, taken prisoner years ago. When he knew that I was an orphan and Lithuanian, he often lured me to his side. He spoke of Lithuania. He comforted my yearning soul with the caress and the music of my native speech and of song. Often he led me to the banks of the gray Niemen, whence I loved to gaze towards the dear hills of my fathers. When we returned to the castle, the old man dried my tears not to awaken suspicion. He dried my tears, and inflamed my vengeance against the Germans. Later, in the years of my youth, I often went with the old man in a boat down to the Lithuanian banks. I plucked my native flowers, and their enchanting scent breathed to my soul some old and dim remembrance. I was a child once more, playing with little brothers in the garden of my parents."

The minstrel teaches him the love of his native

land and a thirst for revenge on those who have wasted it with fire and sword :

" Thou art a slave, and the only weapon of the slave is treachery. Stay still and learn the art of warfare from the Germans. Strive to win their trust to thee."

He does so, and in the next foray escapes to Lithuania. Trained by his enemies, he returns in the course of time to live among them as a traitor, employing against them the arms they have themselves put into his hand.

All this is told at the banquet, where the Knights suppose that they are listening to some romance, and only Konrad knows that it is intended as a spur to rouse him to the action from which his conscience shrinks. He completes the unfinished history. He calls the Knights to arms, and leads them into Lithuania. The inhabitants of the Order's citadel see from the walls the fires of the burning villages glowing on the horizon. The Knights move ever further into the forest fast-nesses of the enemy. Winter comes on, and still the watchers wait in vain for the return of the army. It never returns. A band of stragglers find their way back, bringing as a prisoner the Grand Master who has betrayed them to the Lithuanians. The sentence of death is pronounced upon him. He refuses to die at the hands of his nation's conquerors, and drinks a cup of poison, exulting to the last in the revenge that he has taken for the sake of Lithuania.

" Gaze," is his dying cry, " on the thousands who have perished, on towns in ruins, on homes in flames. Hear ye the hurricane ? It drives before it clouds of snow. The remnants of your ranks freeze there. Hear ye ? The troops of hungry dogs howl there. They quarrel for the morsels of the feast. This is my doing, and I glory in it. As Samson, with one shaking of a pillar, the whole building I destroy, and perish in the fall."

" I will live," says Halban at his side, " to keep the glory of thy deed before the world, to proclaim it to the ages. I will travel through the hamlets, the castles and the towns of Lithuania ; and whither I cannot hasten my song will fly. It shall be as a bard to the knights in battle, and the mother shall sing it for her children in the home. She will sing—and some day in the future from this song shall rise the avenger of our bones."

Such was the cry of Mickiewicz's captive soul that, by a feat of strange daring, he uttered under the eyes of the Russian police. It seems well nigh incredible that it passed the censor ; but it was only after it had been published a year that the authorities saw through the allegory. Then a devoted Russian friend hurried Mickiewicz on a ship bound to Germany. A few hours later, and the poet would have been on his way to Siberia.

The term *Wallenrodism* stands in the Polish language for duplicity of life, the self-defence by cunning and treachery that is enforced by oppression. Yet it is impossible to believe that Mickiewicz advocated a system of national Machiavellism that has never, be it said to her honour, found any favour in the eyes of Poland, or ever formed part of her programme or methods. Such a supposition is irreconcilable with the high moral tendency of Mickiewicz's work for his fellow-Poles, with that of his private life, and with his conception of the sacred function of a poet. He was the first to realize that the course of a Konrad Wallenrod would bring moral death upon the nation that adopted it. That Mickiewicz's countrymen, those for whom he wrote it, whose temper he understood and who understood his as no other can, did not look upon *Konrad Wallenrod* as a summons to base conduct we know. On the contrary, it is a fact that they were inspired to a noble patriotic devotion by a poem, in which the note of Byronism is sunk in a tenderness and passion of love for a lost and unhappy country, that lifts it into the dignity and pathos of a human revelation.

Mickiewicz wrote the epic under the unbearable circumstance of his life in Russia, more as a relief to his own pain than with any definite purpose.* It was written, moreover, as an illustration of the intolerable dilemma forced upon his compatriots. An oppressed nation may be goaded to turn upon a persecutor, not in the open warfare which is forbidden her, but with the underground craft of the fox. Mickiewicz, therefore, sent out in *Konrad Wallenrod* a warning to the conqueror, no less than a cry for sympathy to the Russian people.† Konrad recoils at the thought of the deed he is called upon to perpetrate. His conscience wars against his outraged patriotism. This—its bearing upon the terrible position of the Polish nation—is the tragedy of *Konrad Wallenrod*.

It was in 1829 that Mickiewicz escaped from Russia. Henceforth he could give his inspiration

* M. Zdziechowski, *Byron and His Age*. Cracow, 1897 (Polish).
† Ibid.

its free and full expression. From 1829 till
1832 he wandered between Germany and Italy.
Wherever he went he was followed by the love
and admiration—the worship almost—of those
who came across him. He appears to have possessed
some extraordinary fascination, a power all his
own of winning hearts. To his great genius he
united a captivating simplicity, a single-hearted
straightness and idealism of aim, a large generosity
in dealing with his fellow men. Splendid as were
his mental gifts, mere intellect had no attraction
in his eyes. The fire of the soul, spiritual insight,
the appeal of the heart, were to him the factors
of life that counted.

Mickiewicz was wintering in Rome when, on
the night of November 29th, 1830, the Polish
Rising broke out. It is said that from the hour
the news reached him he never again knew what
it is to feel lightness of heart. Unlike the majority
of his compatriots, who hailed the war as Poland's
certain liberation, Mickiewicz foresaw the worst.
On the eve of the insurrection, racked by pre-
science of what must and did come, he poured
out his grief in his famous poem *To the Polish
Mother*.

" Oh, Polish mother ! when from thy son's
eyes the light of genius shines ; when from his
childish brow the noble pride of the Poles of old
looks forth :

" When, spurning his little band of playmates,
he runs to the aged man who will sing to him his
nation's songs ; when with bowed head he listens
to the history of his sires :

" Oh, Polish mother, ill are these pastimes for

thy son. Kneel thou before the image of the Mother of Dolours, and gaze upon the sword that has transfixed her bleeding heart. With a like blow the foe shall pierce thy bosom.

"Because, though all the world shall bloom in peace; though nations, rulers, minds shall be at one; thy son is called to battle without glory, to martyrdom without a resurrection.

"Then bid him early choose for his musing place a lonely den, where he shall breathe the wet and rotten air, and share his couch with noxious reptiles.

"There shall he learn to hide with anger underground, to make his mind impenetrable as a deep abyss, slowly to poison speech as a putrid exhalation, to bear his cringing form even as a slimy snake.

"Our Saviour, when a child in Nazareth, fondled a little cross on which He saved the world.* Oh, Polish mother! I would fain amuse thy child with his future playthings.

"So must thou early wreathe his little hands with chains, bid him be harnessed to the convict's barrow, so that he shall not pale before the executioner's hatchet or redden to behold the hangman's cord.

"For he shall not go as the knights of old to plant in Jerusalem the victorious cross, nor as the soldiers of a new world to till the field for freedom and water the earth with his life's blood.

"His future challenge will be that of an

---

* The presentment in Italian art of the Blessed Virgin handing a toy cross to the Divine child, of which Mickiewicz saw many examples in a journey he took on the Italian coast shortly before the outbreak of the Rising, was in part the motive of this poem.

unknown spy. A perjured government will wage war with him. A secret dungeon will be his battlefield, and a strong enemy shall pronounce his doom.

" And to the vanquished shall remain the dry wood of the gallows for his tombstone, for all his glory the short weeping of a woman, and the long night talks of his compatriots."

Thus did Mickiewicz mourn for his nation. His sorrow gathers volume till it finds its culminating point in the unfinished *Ancestors*. He wrote it—or rather, he wrote the Third Part—in Dresden, in 1832. With its strange, ghostly atmosphere of the Lithuanian feast of the dead that gives its name to the play, its memories of the comrades of his youth in the Russian prison, its outburst of a Pole's despair, it stands among the greatest creations of national literature.

II

Mickiewicz had written the first, second, and fourth parts of the *Ancestors* when a schoolmaster at Kowno. Steeped in the romantic traditions of Lithuania, he chose the Lithuanian ghost feast of which he had heard from his peasant nurse, and which still lingered here and there in the countryside during his childhood, as the background, first, for the poetical version of his disappointment in love, later, for that of his imprisonment. Hailing from the days of antiquity, the ceremony of the Ancestors was held on All Souls' night in some lonely dwelling adjacent to a cemetery, and in secret to avoid the censure of the priests. Behind barred doors at midnight food was spread for the spirits whom the incantations of the wizard summoned. These rites were characterized by a curious mingling of paganism and the Catholic doctrine on Purgatory.

We are in a chapel on All Souls' night. The doors and windows are fastened and shrouded. The peasants are gathered round the wizard, craving for a sight of their dead.

The wizard cries :

" Souls from Purgatory! Wherever in the world ye be! Ye who burn in flaming pitch! Ye who freeze 'neath beds of rivers! Ye who, for more grievous penance, prisoners in the logs of wood that the flames gnaw on the stoves, weep and whistle mournfully!* Hasten all to this our meeting! Let us all meet here together. Lo, we keep the Ancestors. Come ye to the holy precincts. Here are alms and here are prayers. Here is food and here is drink."

He takes a handful of incense from the peasants.

" I will light it. You shall quickly, when the flamelet shoots on high, drive it with the lightest breathing. Thus, oh, thus, and further, further. Let it burn upon the air."

Then the fluttering of wings breaks through the darkness and silence. The ghosts float in. First, two little children who cannot enter Paradise because they have known no bitterness in life. The wizard lays upon their lips a bitter grain so

---

* According to Polish folk-lore, when the wood on the fire hisses or seems to wail, it is the voice of a soul fulfilling there its Purgatory and begging prayers.

that the entry to heaven is opened to them. At midnight, when the glare of a pitcher filled with flaming brandy sends a lurid light through the chapel, a horrible ghost looks in at the window. He is the cruel master, tortured by those he ill-treated under the shape of birds of prey. Nothing may be given to him because he showed no mercy, and shall find none.

So the phantoms come and go. The cock crows. The rites must end with the dawn. One last spectre enters behind his time. He will utter no word, and only points in silence to his bleeding heart. He is the lover, rejected by one of the women who is present, and who stands for Mickiewicz himself. Whether the wound in Gustavus' heart means that he has literally killed himself, or whether it stands merely for the metaphorical death of his first love, is never made clear.

The Fourth Part is entirely taken up with Gustavus' raving of his betrayal by the girl he loved. He pours it forth to an old man in a lonely cottage. But here again we cannot tell if he is of the spirit world or of ours. As each hour strikes he pauses to count, and when midnight sounds he disappears. This mystery adds its ghostly touch to a play where supernatural visitants hover all about us.

Between these parts and the third many waters had rolled beneath the bridges. Mickiewicz had endured imprisonment and exile. Upon his nation had fallen calamities which, as the poet wrote the Third Part of the *Ancestors*, came near to breaking his heart. Mickiewicz had entered his prison a disappointed lover, to try his soul against the hardest realities of a Pole's life. His love for a woman died in the prison walls, giving place to the master passion of his soul—devotion to his country.

The Third Part is dedicated to the three Philomathians who were the first to die in exile : " To my fellow-students, fellow-prisoners, fellow-exiles, who died of yearning for their country, in Archangel, in Moscow, in Petersburg."

The scene opens in Konrad's prison cell. Konrad, a sort of re-incarnation of Gustavus, is sleeping there. His dreams are troubled. Angels and demons are whispering alternately to his ear as a sign of the moral struggle that is close upon him. He wakes to realize that exile will be his lot. Rising, he writes with a piece of coal on the wall : " D.O.M. Gustavus. Hic natus est Conradus." The Byronic Gustavus, the lover of a woman, is no more. Konrad, the lover of a nation, is born in his stead. It is obvious throughout the play that Mickiewicz puts his own personality into Konrad.

There follows the famous Christmas Eve meeting in the prison. The prisoners, seizing the opportunity of the guard being drunk and abetted by the Polish corporal, an old Napoleonic legionary who is said to be the only fictitious figure of the group, assemble in Konrad's cell by way of making such festivity as they can. This Christmas Eve gathering is not a fiction. It took place in Mickiewicz's cell. The youths, with their strong, brotherly affection, playing the game to the end, chaffing and jesting, striving to keep up their spirits where death or Siberia awaited them, are no creatures of a poet's fancy. They are flesh and blood, Mickiewicz's beloved and lost friends, here under their own names. So strong was the truth with which Mickiewicz portrayed them that one of their band, reading the *Ancestors* in after days, said that he was transported back through the intervening years to the prison as though he had never left it. To the modern reader they seem living companions in a room, not those who have long since gone from this world.

The prisoners meet, greet the new-comers, and exchange conjectures as to their future fate. One of them, Zegota—Mickiewicz's life-long friend, Domeyko—has that day been arrested in the farm in which he takes a youthful landowner's pride, little guessing that he will never see it again. Another has been torn from a young wife. A third cannot tell how long he has languished in a cell where no ray of light ever enters. Zan himself has been half-poisoned by foul food and rank air in a subterranean dungeon. But :

" I would rather be underground there," cries Zan, who, from the beginning, had offered to bear the whole penalty if only his followers might go free. " I would rather be there in hunger and sickness, rather endure flogging and, what is worse than flogging, going before the Commission, than be in a better cell to find you all here."

With what grief and affection, as Mickiewicz wrote these words, must his heart have gone out to Zan, the guide of his youth who, while the poet thus recorded his devotion, was working out its price in Siberia.

In spite of all the efforts after mirth made by Frejend, here, as in reality, the jester and the

musician of the imprisoned Philomathians, the
talk turns to the doom that has already fallen
upon numbers of their comrades and will fall
upon them. One of the prisoners tells how, as he
returned from his examination before the Commission, he saw a procession of the young men and
boys they know starting on their journey to
Siberia.

"The drum gave the signal. The prison was
opened. I saw them. Behind each one walked
guards with a bayonet. Young boys, wasted and
worn, with shaved heads and chains on their legs.
The youngest, a child of ten years, complained
he could not lift up his chain, and showed his bare,
bleeding leg. They brought out Janczewski. He
was disfigured, he had grown haggard, he had
grown thin, but somehow strangely ennobled.
He who, a year ago, had been a mischievous, pretty
little boy, to-day gazed out from his prison cart,
as that emperor gazed from his desert rock,* with
proud, dry and calm eyes. Now he seemed to be
comforting the sharers of his bondage. Now he
bade farewell to the people with a bitter but
gentle smile, as though he would tell them : ' I
do not mind much.' The cart started, they lashed
up the horse. He took his hat from his head, he
stood up, and shouted three times : ' Poland hath
not perished yet.'† They disappeared in the
crowd ; but that hand raised to heaven, that
shaved head, proud, unashamed, that proclaimed
to all its innocence and its disgrace, remained
before my eyes and will remain in my mind, and

* Napoleon.
† The first line of the song of the Polish legions.

on the road of my life they shall be as my compass pointing and leading me to virtue. If I forget them, oh, God in heaven, forget Thou me."

To which his hearers reply by a general Amen. He resumes :

" The other carts had driven up in one long row. They were drawn up one after the other. I cast a glance at the closely pressed throngs of the people. Each face had grown pallid as death. And in that great crowd such was the heavy silence that I heard each step, each clank of the chains. They brought out the last of the prisoners. It looked as if he were resisting, but it was because the poor boy could not walk. He tottered each moment, he staggered slowly down the steps, and hardly had he reached the second step when he fell his whole length. It was Wasilewski. He had been here in the prison near us. The day before yesterday they flogged him so much that not one drop of blood remained in his face."

The soldier, furtively wiping his tears, lifted him into the cart.

" And, as if he had been taken down from the cross, his hands were stretched out on the soldier's shoulders, his eyes terrible, white, wide-opened. And the people opened their lips, and simultaneously one deep, hollow sigh, torn from a thousand breasts, groaned all around as if all the graves groaned under the church. The carts flew down the street like a flash of lightning. One was empty, the prisoner was there, but could not be seen. Only a hand was stretched out to the people from the straw, a hand, livid, wide-open, dead, that quivered as if in farewell."

The story ends, and none of the listeners can speak. Presently they pull themselves together, and sing and make merry. One of them sings a blasphemous song, at which Konrad, for all he declares that he has little faith left, angrily interposes, intimating that he will not allow the name of Mary to be treated with anything but reverence. He sits apart, as he has sat all the evening, brooding and gloomy, till his friends lay hold of him and, with a burst of chaff, insist that he shall improvize to Frejend's flute. This is one of the intimate touches that illustrate how close is the connection of Konrad with his author. Mickiewicz possessed the gift of improvization and, while he was waiting in Wilna for his final sentence, improvized, always accompanied by the flute of that same Frejend.

Konrad flings out a wild song breathing revenge on Russia, for which he is sternly reproved by a priest among the prisoners and by the corporal. He sings on in a poetic frenzy that degenerates into delirium, and ends in a swoon. The corporal gives the alarm that the guard is returning. The prisoners all rush to their cells, leaving Konrad lying unconscious.

Now enters the great moment of the drama. Konrad, alone in his cell, sings the *Improvization*, the most splendid piece of inspiration that Mickiewicz ever reached. On one side, it is the unveiling of the poet's mind at the actual moment of his ecstasy : an Adam waking to life, as in Michelangelo's fresco, at the finger of his creator. On the other, the wounds of the Polish soul that sees his nation suffering, unavenged by either man or

God, are here laid open, bare and bleeding, to the vision.

Konrad is in a dungeon; but what bonds of man's devising can enchain his spirit?

"My songs, ye do not need men's eyes, men's ears! Oh, God, oh, nature, hearken unto me! Worthy of you my music and my song. I am the master! I, the master, stretch forth my hands, I stretch them even to the skies, and lay my hands upon the stars, as on the crystal wheels of an harmonica. Now fast, now slow, as my soul wills, I turn the stars. Millions of sounds flow forth. 'Twixt million sounds each sound I caught, each sound I know. I weave them into rainbows, harmonies, and verse. I pour them forth in music and in lightning streamers.

"I have taken away my hands. I have raised them above the borders of the world, and the harmonica's wheels are held in their flight. Alone I sing. I hear my songs. Long, wailing, as the breathing of the tempest's blast, they moan with grief, they roar with storm, and the ages answer with deep echoings. And each sound together plays and flames. I see each one, I hear each one, as I hear the flight of the wind when, whistling, it rocks the waves, as I see it in its robe of cloud.

"Worthy of God and nature such a song! That song is great, that song is creation, that song is strength, is power, that song is immortality. I feel immortality, I create immortality. What greater couldst Thou do, oh, God?"

Has any other poet, any other wise man, cries he in the rapture of his inspiration, ever felt:

"As I feel to-night, in this lonely night, when

alone I sing within myself, alone I sing unto myself.
Yea, I feel, and I am mighty, and I understand.
To-night is my zenith, to-night is the crisis of
my power. I will cast off my body, and as a spirit
I will take pinions only. I will fly forth from the
turning-wheel of stars and planets, I will reach to
the boundary of the Creator and of nature.

" And I have them, I have them, I have these
two wings. They will suffice. I will strike the past
with the left, the future with the right, and on
the flames of feeling I will come to Thee. And I
will gaze into Thy feeling, oh, Thou, of Whom
they say that Thou feelest in the heavens. I am
here, I have come here, Thou seest what is my
power, my wings reach even here. But I am man,
and my body is there on earth. There did I love,
and in my country hath remained my heart.

" But that love of mine hath not rested on one
man, not on one family, not on one century. I
love a whole nation. I have gathered in my arms
all her past and future generations. I have pressed
her to my bosom as a friend, a lover, a husband, as
a father. I would fain raise her, give her joy. I
have no power to do it—and I have come here to
find it. I have come armed with the whole strength
of thought, that thought which tore Thy thunderbolts from heaven, that tracked Thy planets'
march, and flung open the deep bottom of the
sea. I have more ; I have that power men do not
give, for I have feeling.

" I was born a creator. My powers came whence
came Thine to Thee. Thou hast them, Thou fearest
not to lose them—and I fear not. In the moments
of my strength, when I gaze on high at the trails

of clouds, and hear the wandering birds sailing on wings scarce seen, I will; and with my eye I hold them in the snare. Only corrupted man, weak but immortal, does not serve me, does not know me—does not know us both, Thee and me. Here in heaven I seek the means of ruling him. I would fain wield that power I have on nature over human souls. Not with weapons, not with songs, not with learning, not with miracles. I would fain rule with the feeling that is in me, rule even as Thou rulest over all. Let men be for me as thoughts and words from which a house of song is woven at my will. They say that even thus Thou rulest. Thou knowest that I have not corrupted thought, that I have not squandered speech. If Thou wilt give me a like rule over souls, I will create my nation as a living song, and greater marvels will I work than Thou; I will entone a song of joy. Give me the rule of souls! I would fain have power like Thou possessest. I would fain rule souls even as Thou rulest them."

Here the speaker halts, awaiting God's answer.

Part at least of the extent of Konrad's blasphemy will be made clear when we remember that in Mickiewicz's scheme the brain and understanding cannot be the motive power of the world's salvation. To him the heart, love, feeling, must be the rulers of the human race. The works of the intellect without the heart in the eyes of this man of great mental power stood for brute force, for militarism with all its consequences.

There is silence. Then Konrad cries:

" Thou art silent! Now I know, I have found Thee out. He hath lied who called Thee love.

Thou art only wisdom. With the mind, not with the heart, shall Thy ways be found. Thou hast given the world to thought, and Thou leavest the heart in eternal penance."

The situation now develops its peculiar tragedy. We have seen the poet carried on by lust of power and intellectual pride to defy his Creator. But now that poet merges into the Pole ; the Pole who represents the mental anguish of a nation ; the Pole who has lived among the deep and bitter things of life, who has from his childhood known misery and injustice. Konrad's temptation, said in 1890 the son of Adam Mickiewicz, is the temptation of the whole Polish nation.* Konrad blasphemes, and it is his country's suffering that drives him to his blasphemy. He entreats for power, but for the power that will govern by love in a world ground down by brute strength, the power that will at last entone the hymn of joy for Poland. It is the sorrow of his nation that maddens him, not his own. Mickiewicz's heart nearly broke within him as he uttered this cry of despair. He wrote it in one night. The next morning, he was found lying like Konrad unconscious on the floor of his room.

" Once more I challenge Thee," goes on Konrad, while around him angels and devils battle for his soul. " Thou art silent ? I challenge Thee. Despise me not. I am not alone, although I am raised to these heights alone. On earth my heart is brothered with a great nation. I will wage with Thee a bloodier war than Satan. He fought for the intellect, I challenge for the heart. I have

* L. Mickiewicz, *Life of Adam Mickiewicz.* Posen, 1890 (Polish).

suffered, I have loved, I have grown in torments and in love. When Thou didst tear from me my personal joy, I did not raise my hand against heaven.

" Now is my soul incarnate in my country. I and my country are one. My name is Million, because I love millions and for millions suffer torment. I look on my unhappy land as a son upon his father broken on the wheel. I feel the sufferings of the whole nation as the mother feels within her bosom the sufferings of her child. I suffer, I madden—and Thou, wise and happy, ever rulest, ever judgest, and they say Thou dost not err.

" Hearken ! If that be true which I heard with a son's faith when I came into this world, that Thou lovest ; if Thou, creating it, didst love the world ; if Thou hast a father's heart for what Thou didst create ; if beneath Thy rule love is not a mere anomaly ; if on the millions of men crying ' Help ! ' Thou dost not look solely as on the solution of a complicated sum ; if love is necessary for aught in Thy world and is not only Thy mistaken figure—"

The cries of the angels and demons interrupt him. Then his last entreaty breaks forth :

" Thou art silent ! I have opened the depths of my heart unto Thee. I implore Thee give me power, one small part of power, a part of that which on the earth pride has won. With that small part what joy I would create ! Thou art silent ! Thou wilt not give it to the heart, oh, give it to the brain ! Thou seest that I am the first of men and of the crowd of angels. Worthy I am that Thou shouldst share half of Thy power

with me. If I have not divined Thee right, reply.
Thou art silent, and Thou trustest that Thou
hast a mighty hand. Know that feeling will burn
what the mind will not break. Thou seest that
feeling is my burning-glass.

"Answer me, for I will shoot against Thy
nature ! If I do not overthrow it into ruins, then
I will shake the whole space of Thy dominions.
For I will shoot forth my voice through all the
boundaries of creation, that voice which shall
descend from generations to generations ; I will
cry out that Thou art not the father of the world,
but——."

The voice of the demon puts his thought into
words as he hesitates :

"The Tsar."

We realize the point when we remember that
the Tsar of Mickiewicz's day, Nicholas I, was the
man whose vengeance on Poland was sending
thousands of Polish men and women to hopeless
and lifelong misery.

Hearing the culmination of his blasphemy,
Konrad staggers, then falls in a dead faint. With
wild cries, the demons rush upon him, to claim
their prey.

The key is turned. The corporal enters, accompanied by a friar whom he has fetched, being
disquieted by the sounds he has heard issuing from
Konrad's cell. There before them lies Konrad,
insensible, moaning out broken words.

"The pit . . . a thousand years . . . empty
. . . still more. I shall last out ten thousands of
thousand years. . . . Pray. . . . Here prayer
availeth nought. . . . And was there such a

bottomless and boundless pit? I knew not . . . and there was."

" Thou hearest how he sobs," says the corporal.

" Son," says the priest, who has raised Konrad in his arms, " thou art on a heart that loves thee."

But there is something unusual here, and the priest bids the corporal leave him alone with the prisoner. Then, still unconscious, Konrad, out of his broken heart, sobs out his fathomless despair.

" I see hence, yea, even hence, though it is dark . . . deep. I see thee, Rollison! * Brother! thou, too, art in the prison, scourged, all streaming with blood. And God has not listened to thee, and thou art in despair. Thou seekest a knife, thou tryest to dash thy head against the walls : ' Help!' God does not give it, I cannot give it thee. But I will show thee the way to death. Thou hast a window. Dash it open, leap, leap down, and break thy neck.† And fly with me to the deep, to the dark. Let us fly to the pit, the abyss. That abyss is better than the vale of earth. There, there are no brothers, mothers, nations, tyrants."

The priest perceives that Konrad is in the possession of the demon. He begins the rites of exorcism. The evil spirit, speaking in Konrad's tones, answers in a meaningless and foolish polyglot, till the friar drives him forth. Konrad wakes.

" Dost thou raise me? Who art thou? Beware lest thou thyself shalt fall into this pit. He gives me his hand. Let us fly! Like a bird I fly to the heights. I breathe sweet scents, I shine

---

* A fellow-prisoner who has been flogged in another cell.
† Here again Mickiewicz draws on a real incident. One of his brother prisoners flung himself from his window.

with light. Who gave me his hand? Good men and angels. Whence your pity that for me descended to this pit? Men? I despised men, the angels I have not known."

"Pray," answers the priest, "for the hand of the Lord hath terribly touched thee. The lips with which thou hast outraged the Eternal Majesty, those lips the evil spirit hath polluted with hideous words. God grant that the words of folly, heaviest punishment for the learned lips, be counted as thy penance, God grant thou shalt forget them."

Konrad: "They are there—hammered in."

The Priest: "God grant, oh, sinner, that thou thyself shalt never more decipher them, that God shall never ask thee an account of them."

He kneels, as Konrad falls asleep. "Thy mercy, Lord, is without bounds," he cries. Prostrating himself on the ground, he implores the divine forgiveness, offering himself as a victim in expiation of Konrad's sin. Even as on the Christmas Eve which Mickiewicz and his companions spent in Adam's prison cell, they heard the Polish Christmas carols ringing out from a church near by, which, says a fellow-prisoner of the poet, "transported us to our firesides where our mothers and sisters were weeping for us";* so now into the dungeon where the priest and prisoner are alone penetrates the music of these hymns. Above them resound the voices of alternate choirs of angels, crying the one for mercy, the other for justice, on the sinner.

* Ignacy Domeyko, *The Philaretians and Philomathians*, quoted by L. Mickiewicz, *Life of Adam Mickiewicz*.

The first archangel : " Oh, Lord, he hath sinned, he hath grievously sinned against Thee."

The second archangel : " But Thy angels are weeping for him, Thy angels are praying for him."*

The first archangel : " Tread down, oh, Lord, break to fragments, oh, Lord, those who despise Thy holy decrees."

The second archangel : " But forgive those who have not understood Thy holy decrees."

An angel : " When, flying with the star of hope, I shone upon Judea, the angels sang the hymn of birth. The wise men saw us not. Kings hearkened not to us. But shepherds saw, and ran to Bethlehem. Poor, simple, lowly men first welcomed the Eternal wisdom, and owned the Eternal rule."

The first archangel : " When the Lord saw pride and craft in the hearts of His servant archangels, the Lord did not forgive the eternal spirits, the pure angels. Bands of angels fell like a rain of stars from the heavens, and the rain of the minds of learned men fall with them every day."

The second archangel : " He did not search into Thy decrees as one curious to know. Nor was it for human wisdom that he sought, nor yet for fame."

The first archangel : " He knew Thee not, he revered Thee not, oh, our great Lord. He did not love Thee, he did not call upon Thy name, oh, our Redeemer."

* This is said to refer to the prayers of two Polish girls with whom Mickiewicz had formed a close spiritual intimacy when in Rome. With the one of these who lives in his poetry as Eva, he fell in love, but the opposition of the father intervened, and they never married.

The second archangel : " But he honoured the name of Thy most holy Mother. He loved a nation, he loved much, he loved many."

Both choirs of archangels : " Lift Thou his head. He shall arise from the dust, he shall reach to the heavens, and of his own will he will fall and honour the cross. May the whole world with him prostrate itself at the foot of the cross; and let it praise Thee for Thy justice and Thy mercy, our Lord and our God."

Thus Mickiewicz's *Ancestors* rises above the mere sceptical drama. Love saves the sinner. The heart breaks down the barrier of intellectual pride. Heaven replies to Konrad's agonized appeal; but not by language that could convince his reason : rather by the charity that sought the blasphemer in his cell, that drove the demon forth, that took upon itself the penalty.

The remainder of the incomplete Part III. is only connected by the slenderest of threads with what has passed. Konrad leaves the scene until the closing episode is reached. One link binds the drama together—Poland's sufferings and the supernatural presences with their power on the soul for good or ill. The maiden, who is the idealization of Mickiewicz's love for " Eva," prays for the prisoner unknown to her, and beholds a vision of angels which, with its grace and lightness, breaks into the stern tragedy of the *Ancestors* like a strain of celestial music. On the other hand, the vision of the friar that immediately follows it, with no apparent connection, is entirely national.

es, and he cries out in horror :

see I ? Long, white, the course of the

highway. Long are those roads we cannot see, o'er wastes, o'er snows, all leading to the north. There, there to a distant land like streams they flow. They flow. Straight runs that road to a gate of iron. See! o'er those roads is rushing a band of carts, like clouds driven by the winds. All to one goal. Ah, Lord, those are our youths who go there to the north. Lord, Lord, exile is their fate! And wilt Thou suffer them all to perish in their youth? And wilt Thou destroy our generation to the end?"

He foretells Poland's salvation by a child who will grow to be her defender, her restorer, whose name "shall be forty and four. Lord, wilt Thou not deign to hasten his advent, to comfort my nation?" He sees that nation arraigned at the world's tribunal as a Christ: and all this passage, likening Poland to the Christ of the nations, dying as Christ on the Cross for humanity, victorious before all eyes, is Messianism in one of its most pronounced forms. The vision ends by the friar beholding the white robe of Poland clothing the whole universe, as she, whom he fondly calls his beloved, ascends to heaven and to her glory. Then again rises before his thought the same mysterious saviour, the "vicegerent on the vale of earth, blind, but led by an angel page, the man of three faces whose footstool is three cities, at whose call three ends of the world tremble. He, himself, is uncrowned, though he stands over kings and peoples. And his life is toil of toils, and his name forty and four."

What is the clue to this allusion we do not know. Was that restorer of the nation a curious foreshadowing of the advent of the mystic Towianski to whose spiritual authority Mickiewicz gave himself up for years of his life, and from whom he expected the regeneration of humanity ? The threefold face is said to refer to the triple message that Towianski considered himself empowered from on high to bring to Slavonia, France, and Israel. It is a fact, moreover, that Towianski was in his youth blind as the man of the friar's dream. Or it has been suggested from a play on the Roman figures that forty-four stands for Louis Napoleon, who at one time seemed prepared to deliver Poland. But these are conjectures, and we have no means of interpreting what was passing in a mind so strongly impregnated with mysticism as Mickiewicz's. In moments of exaltation Mickiewicz uttered things that are not possible to explain by ordinary laws.

Next come the dreams of Novosiltzov, and these are horrible nightmares provoked by demons. The scene shifts to the Warsaw salons where the talk runs on what is happening in Lithuania. Here one of the guests tells the history of his friend Cichowski. The strong simplicity of the language in which Mickiewicz relates this story adds to the pity of its tragedy. I cannot attempt to present this celebrated passage in anything more than a prose translation which, while giving no conception of the art of Mickiewicz's poem, will, at least, reproduce its facts.

" I knew him when I was a child. He was young then, lively, witty, and gay, famous for his good looks. He was the life of the company. He amused everyone with his stories and jokes. He loved children, and took me often on his knee. Then he married. I remember that he brought to us children presents from his betrothed, and invited us to his wedding. Then for a long time he never came, and it was said in my home that he had disappeared, no one knew where. The government sought for him, but could find out no trace of him. At last it was said that he had killed himself, that he was drowned. The police found his cloak on the banks of the Vistula. They brought the cloak to his wife. She recognized it. He was dead. They did not find his body—and so a year passed away. Why did he kill himself? This was asked, was inquired into. He was mourned, he was wept for. Finally, he was forgotten. And two years went by. One evening they were taking prisoners to the Belvedere from another prison. The evening was rainy and dark. Some one, whether by chance or on purpose, was a spectator of this procession. Perhaps it was one of the brave youths of Warsaw who keep a watch on the whereabouts and names of the prisoners. Patrols were in the streets, dead silence in the town. Then someone cried out from behind a wall: ' Prisoners, who are you? ' A hundred names answered. Among them his name was heard: and the next day his wife was told. She wrote and she ran, she begged, she implored; but she heard nothing save that one name. And again three years passed on with no trace, with no news. But, in some unknown way, it was spread through Warsaw that he was alive, that he was being tortured, that he refused to tell anything, and that so far he had told nothing; that for many nights they would not allow him to sleep ; that they fed him on herrings and gave him nothing to drink ; that they drugged him with opium, and sent horrible apparitions and monsters upon him ; that they tickled his soles and his armpits. But soon other prisoners were taken, the talk began about others. Only his wife wept, all the others forgot.

" Till, not long ago, they rang at his wife's house one night. The door was opened. An officer and a gendarme, armed, and a prisoner. It was he ! They ordered pen and paper for him to sign that he had returned alive from the Belvedere. They took the note, and threatened him with their fingers : ' If you let out . . . . ' and they did not finish. They went as they came. It was he. I ran to see him. A friend warned me, ' Do not go to-day, for you will find a spy at the gate.' The next day I went. There were the soldiers of the police in the hall. I went in a week's time. It was he who would not receive me : he was ill. Then, not long ago, I met him driving outside the town. They told me it was he, for I did not know him. He had grown fat, but it was a horrible fatness. He was swollen by bad food and poisonous air. His cheeks were puffy, yellow, and pale. His forehead was wrinkled as if he were half a century old; he had lost all his hair. I bade him welcome. He did not know me. He did not wish to speak to me. I told him who I was. He looked at me without seeing me. When I spoke of the details of our old acquaintance, he fixed his eyes inquiringly on me. Ah ! all that he had suffered in his torments by day and all that he had thought through in his sleepless nights, I knew it all in that one minute from his eyes.

" In a month's time I went again. I thought
that by then he would have been able to look
about in the world, and to call back his memory.
But he had been so many thousand days under
the ordeal of the inquisition, so many thousand
nights he had communed alone with himself, so
many years tyrants had carried on the inquiry by
torture, so many years he had been surrounded
by walls that had ears, when his only defence was
silence, and his only companion darkness, that a
gay city could not blot out in one month the
lesson of so many years. To him the sun is a spy,
the day his traducer, his servants his jailors, each
guest is his enemy. If a visitor comes to his house,
at the sound of the bolt being unshot, he immediately thinks : ' They are coming for the inquisition.' He turns his back, he leans his head on
his hand. It appears he is gathering together his
presence of mind, all the powers of his brain. He
compresses his lips, so that no words shall escape
them. He casts down his eyes that the spies may
guess nothing from his eyes. If the visitors ask
him a question, he, still believing he is in prison,
rushes to the other end of the room, and escapes
there in the shadows, crying out always two
phrases : ' I know nothing. I shall say nothing.'
And these two phrases are his watchword. And
his wife and child weep long on their knees before
him, till he can conquer his fear and his horror."

We pass back again to Wilna : to Novosiltzov,
giving a banquet, spurning the blind mother, as
she implores him to let her visit her prisoner son
who is being flogged to death, and whose fate
haunted Konrad as he lay unconscious. But where

all this time is Konrad ? The friar has stood before Novosiltzov warning him that upon him and his ministers God's vengeance is about to fall—and it is a fact that sudden death and disaster overtook the prime movers in the persecution of the Lithuanian youths. On his way from Novosiltzov's rooms, the priest meets Konrad, who is being conducted by soldiers to his examination. Konrad stops and gazes, bewildered. He believes he has never seen the priest as a living man. It must have been in a dream that the friar came to his aid. He hails him therefore as the friend of a dream, and thanks him for a gift of which, so he thinks, only his own conscience is aware.

" Thou shalt go," says the priest, " on a far and an unknown road. Thou wilt be in the crowd of the great, the rich, the learned. Seek thou the man who knoweth more than they. Thou wilt know him, for he will be the first to greet thee in the name of God."

This is supposed to be a further reference to Towianski.

" What is this ? " cries Konrad, struck by the familiar sound of the voice that had consoled him in the hour of his agony. " Is it thou ? What may this be ? Stop a moment for the love of God."

" Farewell, I cannot," replies the priest ; and Konrad is hurried off by the soldiers.

His next and last entry into the strange, mystic drama is shrouded in the veils of mystery. The feast of the Ancestors is being held again as in the beginning of the play. The wizard and the woman whom Gustavus loved are in the cemetery. The woman entreats the phantom that appeared with his bleeding heart in the past to show himself to her once more. The songs of the incantations are wafted to their ears. Graves open. Spirits float about them. Only the lover does not come. The hour of cock-crow is here. The night of the Ancestors is run. The two who watch cry in vain upon the name of Gustavus.

" Thy lover," says the wizard, " hath either changed the faith of his fathers, or hath changed his old name. See how the dawn draws nigh. The wizard's powers are gone. Thy lover will not come."

But from the west a band of prison carts appears amidst clouds of snow, rushing to the north. The lover is there. He turns back to gaze— only once, but what a look is that farewell to Lithuania ! His heart is bleeding with a thousand wounds which have now entered his soul—the wounds of his country, which death only can heal. On his forehead he carries a black stain which, says the wizard, even death may not cure —his self-inflicted wound, his blasphemy.

" Ah, great God, cure him," cries Gustavus' love ; and the play ends.

To the irreparable loss of literature, the drama was never finished. Mickiewicz intended to have brought it down to the events following the Rising of 1830, and to have developed the action in the Russian prisons and Siberia. His poetic genius was tragically silenced, and the *Ancestors* stands as a magnificent and incomplete monument to the sufferings of Poland. " I read the poem on my knees," wrote Bohdan Zaleski. " Since the tears and the imprecations of the prophets of Sion," so said George Sand, " no voice has been raised with a like power to sing a subject as vast as that of a nation's fall."

III

Shortly after Mickiewicz had written the Third Part of the *Ancestors*, he joined the Polish Emigration in Paris. From that date, 1832, his home was in Paris for the rest of his life, with the exception of the year and a half—1839 to 1840—when he held the chair of Latin Literature at the University of Lausanne. He devoted himself to the exiles and outcasts of his nation. He laboured for them without stint, giving ungrudgingly out of his own dire poverty, harbouring the homeless when he himself could scarcely keep a roof above his head, conferring strength and consolation, not only by his written word, but by the moral force of his life and by his rare gift of influence over the souls of others. He became the chief moral leader of his people and the object of their impassioned affection. He taught them that only by personal regeneration could they hope to see their country restored ; that true patriotism must reform the individual to secure the nation's redemption. For the guidance of his fellow exiles he wrote the *Book of the Polish Pilgrimage*. Mickiewicz had a deep-seated conviction that Poland was the chosen emissary of the higher future of mankind, and that therefore her sons were to be the apostles of the future. It thus followed that

the Polish Emigration was a providential means of
spreading the new light over the face of the world.
The Polish exiles were, therefore, exiles no more,
but pilgrims. They must prove themselves worthy
of that calling. So in his *Book of the Polish Pilgrimage*
he puts together in a species of Biblical
prose a string of counsels for the Polish pilgrim.
Material strength meant little to a man like
Mickiewicz. The power of the idea was everything.
It mattered nothing that at the moment
he wrote this book no visible sign of Poland's
resurrection could be discerned on the political
horizon. He believed with full confidence that the
moment of her triumph and the consequent
spiritual rebirth of the universe was approaching.

It is on these lines that his instructions for the
Polish exiles run: worded in pithy aphorisms, or
in parables.

"The greatness and the strength of the war-
ships are good, but without stars and the compass
they are nought. And the star of the pilgrimage
is heavenly faith, and the magnetic needle is the
love of your country. The star shineth for all,
and the needle pointeth ever to the north. And
of a surety, with that needle, we may sail on the
eastern and western seas, and without it even on
the northern sea there will be wandering and
shipwreck."

"Why has the power of resurrection been given
to your nation ? Not because she was powerful,"
like Rome, nor wise as Greece, glorious as Venice
and Genoa, for they have all fallen and will not
rise again. "But you will be woken from the
grave, as having faith, hope, and love."

" Polish pilgrim, thou wast rich, and lo ! thou sufferest poverty and need, that thou mayest know what are poverty and need, and that when thou returnest to thy country thou shalt say : ' The poor and needy are my co-heirs.' "

Wisdom is not with the great ones of this earth. It has been lost from public life. " And the wise among you," cries he whose soul was on fire with hunger and thirst for the things that make for righteousness, " are not those who have enriched themselves selling their learning, and have bought for themselves goods and houses, and have won gold and favours from kings : but they who have announced to you the word of freedom, and have suffered imprisonment and rods. And they who shall seal their doctrine with their death shall be blessed."

Then must the pilgrim of the country to which Mickiewicz looked for the world's spiritualization, the unarmed pilgrim face to face with the governments of Europe, take heart, for a few poor fishermen were victorious over Rome. Let the Polish pilgrims beware of confounding civilization in its ordinary signification—the cult of the luxury and materialization that have overspread Europe —with the higher civilization of Christian selfsacrifice. They must not be overwhelmed by the strength that lies behind that so-called civilization ; for it is their lot to inculcate upon the nations that have lost all faith, and whose only god is gross materiality, the civilization of Christ. Malaria in a fever-stricken district must be stamped out by searching for its cause. The man who sits at home, instead of leaving it to fight against evil, will be attacked by that evil in his own dwelling-place.

The deadliest foes of the Polish nation are not those who destroyed Poland, but the worshippers of power and interest. The talent of the Pole is not for himself : all must be given to his country. High posts, official dignities, earthly lordships, what are these for the Poles among whom there must be brotherly love alone ?

" In your pilgrimage in a strange country you are as the people of God in the desert." Those who complained, even in the secret of their heart, perished without seeing the promised land. " So beware ye of the sin of lamentation and doubt, that you shall not lengthen the days of your pilgrimage." And that Pole who does not believe in the resurrection of Poland shall be banished, till he repents, from the ranks of the pilgrimage.

" As in the city of the Jews, Christ and His religion arose, so in the cities of Europe will arise your religion, the new religion of self-sacrifice and love."

" The nations shall be redeemed by the merits of a martyred nation, and shall be re-christened in the name of God and liberty. And who is thus christened shall be your brother."

" Sow ye the seed of the love of your country and the spirit of self-sacrifice, and be ye sure that the Republic will grow forth mighty and fair. . . . Truly I say unto you inquire not what the government in Poland will be. It is enough for you to know that it will be better than any of which you know. Nor ask as to her boundaries, for they will be greater than ever before. And each of you has in his soul the seed of the future laws and the measure of the future boundaries. For inasmuch as you make your soul greater and better, so much will you better your laws and increase your boundaries."

These extracts may give some general impression of what is not the most poetical, but one of the frankest expressions of Polish Messianism. The poet finished his book of rules for the pilgrim with a cry from his heart, the prayer and the litany of the Pole.

"Lord God, Who canst do all things ! The children of a warrior nation lift up to Thee their disarmed hands from all the ends of the world. They cry to Thee from the depths of the mines of Siberia and from the snows of Kamchatka,* and from the deserts of Algeria, and from France, a foreign land. But in our own fatherland, in Poland, faithful to Thee, they may not call upon Thee ; and our old men, our women, and our children pray to Thee in secret with their thoughts and tears. God of the Jagiellos !† God of Sobieski ! God of Kościuszko ! have pity on our country and on us. Grant us to pray again to Thee as our fathers prayed, on the battlefield with weapons in our hands, before an altar made of drums and cannons, beneath a canopy of our eagles and our flags. And grant that our families may pray in the churches of our towns and hamlets, and our

---

* Kamchatka is a convict settlement for the Poles. The reference to Algeria is explained by the large number of Poles who since the days of Napoleon served in the French Foreign Legion.

† The Jagiello line of sovereigns under whom Poland attained to her greatest power.

children on our graves. But not our will but Thine be done."

"God the Father," run the supplications in his litany, "Who didst lead Thy people forth from the captivity of Egypt and didst restore them to the Holy Land, restore us to our native land.

"God the Son, Redeemer, Who wast tortured and crucified, Who didst rise again from the dead and Who dost reign in glory, raise our country from the dead.

"Mother of God, whom our fathers called the queen of Poland and of Lithuania, save Poland and Lithuania . . .

"From Russian, Austrian and Prussian bondage, deliver us, oh, Lord. By the martyrdom of thirty thousand knights of Bar, who died for faith and freedom, deliver us, oh, Lord.* By the martyrdom of twenty thousand citizens of Praga, slaughtered for faith and freedom, deliver us, oh, Lord. By the martyrdom of the youths of Lithuania, slain by the knout, dead in the mines and in exile, deliver us, oh, Lord. By the wounds, tears and sufferings of all Polish prisoners, exiles, and pilgrims, deliver us, oh Lord.

"For a universal war for the freedom of the nations, we beseech Thee, oh, Lord. For the national arms and eagles, we beseech Thee, oh, Lord. For a happy death on the field of battle, we beseech Thee, oh, Lord. For a grave for our bones in our own earth, we beseech Thee, oh,

* The Confederation of Bar, headed by Casimir Pulawski, fought Russia for four years (1768-1772), in defence of their country's existence.

Lord. For the independence, integrity and freedom of our country, we beseech Thee, oh, Lord."

Mickiewicz's last and greatest poem followed
the *Book of the Pilgrimage* by two years ; but, in
order not to interrupt the narrative that yet
remains of the rest of the poet's life, I will return
to *Thaddeus* later. Poverty, domestic griefs,
sorrow for his nation, an endless yearning to behold
his native land again ; such is the private history
of Adam Mickiewicz. Moments came when he
and his wife were almost starving. Yet through
all he maintained an unshaken composure of soul,
the confidence in Providence of one to whom the
unseen matters more than the vicissitudes of
earth.

Before Mickiewicz moved to Lausanne, and
again after he returned to Paris to take up the
professorship of Slavonic literature at the Collège
de France, madness fell upon his wife.

During his first year at the Collège, Mickiewicz compared each of his lectures to a hard-
fought battle. In the intervals of tending his wife
in her paroxysms of insanity he prepared the
lectures, on which his family of young children
depended for their maintenance, as best he might
out of a mind racked with suffering. Weighed
down by the tribulation of his home and the
national sorrows that had by now driven all joy
from his heart, he stood before his audience in
which sat the most brilliant men and women in
Paris, his sad face worn and wearied, but with the
fire behind it leaping forth whenever he spoke of
the nation he loved. In the summer of 1841, his
domestic troubles reached their climax, and it

was found necessary to remove his wife to a mad-house.

On his return from accompanying his wife to the asylum, Mickiewicz sat alone in his desolate home, broken with grief. A stranger from Lithuania entered his room. He told Adam that he had words of great import, that he was endowed with a message from God that should save both the human race and their country, and that as a proof of what he said he was able to cure the poet's wife. In grievous doubt, Mickiewicz spent the night wrestling with his conscience as to whether he should accept the leading of this man, Andrew Towianski, or no. He decided finally to go with Towianski to the asylum. The result was that his wife was restored to health, probably by a species of magnetism, and that Mickiewicz became the chief apostle of the mystic system inaugurated by the new prophet.

The scope of this book does not permit me to dwell upon this episode of Mickiewicz's life, or upon the personality and teaching of the mystic Towianski, which latter have been a fruitful subject for controversy. I have told the story more fully in a different place.* Suffice it to say that, with a whole-hearted faith in Towianski's mission, Mickiewicz sacrificed poetic genius, position, friendship. Since the hour that he fell in with Towianski, the creator of the *Ancestors* and *Thaddeus* could never again enrich the literature of his mother-tongue with his splendid poetry. His lectureship in the Collège de France became a pulpit for his mysticism. His adherence to Towianism lost him

* See my *Adam Mickiewicz, the National Poet of Poland.*

this, his last remaining, self-expression and only means of livelihood, for, part of the Towianskian doctrines being a semi-deification of Napoleonism, the French Government expelled him from his chair. For the best years of his manhood he gave himself up to the propagation of a neurotic form of mysticism because he believed it would bring salvation to Poland and the human race. Before his death he emerged from the ordeal of a religion that exacted of its followers a perpetual state of ecstasy, prematurely aged, broken by spiritual strain ; but with his moral grandeur unimpaired. None of the bitter disillusions and disappointments that dogged his life could ever weaken his hope in the resurrection of his nation or his faith in the ideal. He died as he had lived, a sacrifice for his country, his last hours spent in her service. During the Crimean War, he went to Constantinople to organize a Polish legion to fight for Turkey. Filled with sadness at the failure of this enterprise on which he had built a patriot's dream, he was stricken down by Asiatic cholera, and died on November 26th, 1855. A Polish village in the outskirts of Constantinople bears his name, and his memory still lingers in the capital of Turkey. His mortal remains now lie in Cracow among the dead whom his nation honours most.

IV

Thaddeus (1834) is as great a national expression as the *Ancestors*, albeit under a different aspect. Artistically it is Mickiewicz's masterpiece. Where the *Ancestors* is the tragedy of a nation and of the soul suffering in that nation's suffering, *Thaddeus* is an idyll of the Lithuania that Mickiewicz had lived in as a boy, told by the pen of one who had loved and lost her.

The poem, said to be the finest epic of the nineteenth century, runs into twelve cantos. The finished beauty and brilliance of the style, its magnificent word-paintings of nature, were alone enough to give it the place it holds in the history of Poland's literature. But, apart from this, it has always spoken directly to Polish sympathies.

There is scarcely any plot in the story. A Lithuanian boy—the Thaddeus who gives his name to the poem—returns to the country house of his uncle Soplica, after completing his studies. A sort of hereditary feud concerning the right over a ruined castle is dragging on between this family and another, of whom the last representative is a sentimental young Count, a lover of French fashions and of the pseudo romanticism of his day. The quarrel is more nominal than real ; but a more serious question is behind it. The father of Thaddeus, Jacek, was in his youth a suitor for the hand of Horeszko's daughter, whom Mickiewicz, in memory of his own love, calls Eva. His suit was rejected, according to the old Polish custom, by a dish of dark soup being handed to him at the table of the lady's father. In a fury of revenge, he took to a wild life, and seized the moment of the Russian attack on the Horeszko mansion during Kościuszko's rising to shoot the magnate dead. He then fled abroad, fought by way of reparation in the Polish legions for Napoleon, and became a Bernardine monk. Under the cowl and a feigned name he, through the poem, serves as a national emissary from the Polish legions to Lithuania. The Count, the last remaining male scion of the Horeszko family, is urged on by the old retainer of the latter to fight it out with the Soplicas. In the Lithuania of old, where there were no police to enforce the decision of the courts, the pleader had recourse to the nobles, who summoned their armed friends and the private armies that the more powerful of them had at their disposal, and, with a legal officer in their number, marched on the offender to exact justice. The Count leads a like movement against the Soplicas. While they are at blows with each other, the Russians fall upon both with the result that the Poles unite against their common foe. Thaddeus and the Count go off to enrol themselves under the banners of the Polish legions. They return with Napoleon's armies on that march to Moscow, which the Poles hailed as the herald of their country's resurrection. Every quarrel is reconciled, and, with Thaddeus' marriage to the granddaughter of the murdered Horeszko, the family feud and the poem are happily ended.

Such is the outline of *Thaddeus:* but its power and its charm lie in the wealth of its national colouring, the vividness with which Mickiewicz reproduced the types of his youth that, even when he wrote the work, had gone for ever, the magnificent descriptions of nature in wild and romantic Lithuania, all set to the patriotic hope that filled Poland in the last days of Napoleon's glory. Men of a dead past rise again as though in the flesh, with their picturesque, many-coloured, semi-Oriental costume, their hospitable ways, their hunting and shooting in the forest, their open-air and simple, joyous country life. When the sun goes down, work on the estate ends too ; for the master of the mansion ordains that " the Lord of the world knows how long we must work. When the sun, His day-labourer, departs from the sky, it is time for the husbandman to withdraw from the field." So, at sunset, there is a long procession streaming home from the forest and meadows ; servants, labourers, horses, sheep, and oxen with bells at their necks, and the guests and inmates of the house, walking according to precedence in the order that the master decrees. The guest of honour, the " Chamberlain "—the Polish manor was a miniature court with corresponding titles—as, at each meal, he takes the place of honour, " bowed to the ladies, the old men and youths." Manners have a patriarchal simplicity strongly dashed with a quaint ceremonial and punctilious courtesy.

The effect of *Thaddeus* is that of a blessed tranquillity, glorified, as the poem ends, with the promise of the nation's deliverance. It was written for those Poles among whom the poet's exile was passed and whose sorrows he shared, in order to transport their minds from the carking cares, we might in truth say the horrors, that surrounded them. Respite from their troubles could but be known, says the poet—in lines discovered after his death and intended as an introduction to *Thaddeus*—in the " only land in all the past and all the future, where the Pole can find one spark of joy ; the country of our childish years." Overwhelmed with grief for Poland and in the fresh agony of bereavement at the death of his dearest friend, Mickiewicz wrote a poem that is, as Dr. Kallenbach expresses it, eternally young.* At the thought of the tears and blood in which his nation was drowned, he confesses he could find no heart to sing of anything except of things that are tender and serene.

Yet the note of mourning is not entirely absent from *Thaddeus*. The yearning of the exile that tore Mickiewicz's soul till his life ended cannot be wholly kept under. It breaks out again and again, mingling with the sighs of the forest and the cries of the marsh birds which the poet might hear no more.

"Lithuania, my country," are the first words of his Lithuanian epic. " Thou art as health. How to prize thee he only can tell who hath lost thee. To-day the whole charm of thy beauty I see and I sing, for I pine after thee.

"Holy Virgin, who dost guard bright Czenstochowa, † and who shinest over the Ostrian gate," he continues in the invocation that is one of his famous passages, and which was pronounced over his coffin when laid in foreign soil.‡ " Thou who dost defend the castled town of Nowogródek with her faithful people ! Even as by a miracle

---

* J. Kallenbach, *Adam Mickiewicz.*

† The famous Polish shrine of the Blessed Virgin. In these latter days this spot, so peculiarly sacred to Polish national and religious feeling, has been desecrated, as we know, by the presence of the Kaiser and his Prussian hordes, who committed there outrages that are unnamable.

‡ Mickiewicz's remains rested in Paris till 1890 when they were removed to Cracow.

thou didst restore me when a child to health, when by my weeping mother I was offered to thy protection, and I opened my dying eyes, and went on foot to thy shrine to thank God for my recovered life : even so thou wilt restore us by a miracle to the bosom of our land ! Till then, carry my yearning soul to those wooded hills, those green meadows stretching wide on the blue Niemen's shores ; to those fields painted with many-hued grains, golden with wheat, silver with rye ; where grow the amber rape and buck-wheat, white as snow, where with a maiden blush the medick flames."

In the heat and glare of the Paris pavements, the son of a wild, spacious country, to whom a noisy city was always insupportable, remembered with longing the breath of his native forests, the sounds of the Lithuanian evening.

" The sky seemed ever to droop and draw nearer the earth till, both shrouded 'neath a dark veil, like lovers they began secret talk, pleading their loves with faint sighings, with whispers and murmurs and half-uttered words, whence arose the enchanting music of night.

" In the field the evening concert had scarcely begun. Now the musicians began to tune up. Then the landrail screamed three times, the first violin of the meads. Then afar in the marshes the bitterns reply on the bass. Then the snipes, as they rise and they wheel, cry again and again like the beating of little drums.

" As the *finale* to the murmurs of flies and the clamour of birds, the two ponds answer with double choirs, like the Caucasian mountain lakes that, enchanted, are silent by day and play in the night. One pond, transparent of wave and sandy of shore, gave out from its deep blue breast a low, solemn sigh. The other pond, with its muddy depths and its troubled voice, replied with a cry of passion and grief. In both of the ponds sang numberless hordes of frogs, both choirs united in two great chords. One sang *fortissimo*, but the other softly was warbling. One seemed to complain, but the other one only to sigh. Thus, over the fields, did the two ponds converse with each other like two Aeolian harps alternately playing." (*Thaddeus*, Book VIII.)

Another time it is the music of the buffalo horn, wielded by the *Wojski*,* that the poet describes, ringing through glade and thicket.

" He played. The horn, as a blast of wind, on its eddying breath carried music into the depths of the forest, and the echoes repeated the sound. The hunters were dumb, the prickers stood still, amazed at the power and the pureness and the strange harmony of those strains. He filled, he gave life to the woods and the oaks. 'Twas as though he let the dogs loose and started the chase, for there rang in his playing the whole tale of the chase. First, a ringing glad call, the reveille. Then growls, and, after growls, whining, the cries of the dogs. And here and there sharper notes as of thunder—the shots.

" Here he ceased, but the horn went on. All thought that the *Wojski* was playing still, but it was the echo that played.

---

* An old title of office surviving from the independent days of the Republic.

" And again he blew. You would think that the horn changed shape, and that 'twixt the *Wojski's* lips it waxed and it waned, feigning cries of the beasts. Now, long drawn as the voice of the wolf, it howled long and shrill. Again, it spread widely its throat, and roared like a bear. Then the wind gave out the urus' cry.

" Here he ceased, but the horn went on. All thought that the *Wojski* was playing still, but it was the echo that played. Oaks repeated the sound to the oaks, and the beech to the beech.

" Again he blew; and it seemed as though in the horn a hundred other horns played. You heard the confused, mingled noise of the chase, of anger, of fear, of the hunters, the dogs, and the quarry, till the *Wojski* lifted the horn on high, and the hymn of triumph smote on the skies.

" Here he ceased, but the horn went on. All thought that the *Wojski* was playing still, but it was the echo that played. All the trees in the forest were so many horns that carried the song to each other, as from choirs unto choirs. And the music travelled ever wider, ever farther, ever softer, ever purer, ever perfect, till it died far, far, somewhere far off on the threshold of heaven." (*Thaddeus*, Book IV.)

Mickiewicz is a master of the Polish language. The natural richness of the Polish tongue, its peculiar delicacies of word shading, its onomatopœia that is one of its chief characteristics, are handled by Mickiewicz with the skill of a musician whose instrument obeys his every call. The sounds of the woodland life of Lithuania, the roaring of the tempest through the forests, the whisper of the wind over meadows and marshes, the cries of bird and beast, fill the pages of *Thaddeus* with the harmonies of a wild and romantic land.

"My native trees!" he says in one place, hailing the giants of the forest whose age was as long as time. "If Heaven grant I shall return to gaze on you, my friends of old, shall I still find you? Are you still living? Ye, around whom I wandered once, a child.

"How much I owe you, oh, my native trees! I, a poor shot, escaping from the mockery of my friends for my missed quarry, how often, in your stillness, I hunted dreams when, in the wild hunting grounds, I forgot the chase and sat me on a log. And around me the earth was silver with the hoary-bearded moss mingled with the deep blue of black and rotten berries. And, further, flamed heathery knolls decked with red berries, like a rosary's coral beads. All darkness round me. Branches swung on high like green, thick, drooping clouds. Somewhere above their tranquil arch the gale raved, wailing, roaring, howling, crashing, thundering. Strange deafening uproar! It seemed that overhead was rocking a roaring sea." (*Thaddeus*, Book IV.)

While the ear is satisfied in *Thaddeus*, the eye dwells on the pageantry of sunset and sunrise on the marshes, on the storm sweeping over the wide Lithuanian skies. As a painter of nature, exquisite and true to detail, Mickiewicz stands unrivalled in his native literature. There are few, says Dr. Kallenbach, his equal in any literature.* Such is the veracity of his descriptions that a Pole whom

* J. Kallenbach, *Adam Mickiewicz.*

years of exile had separated from his country could say : " I read *Thaddeus* aloud, and often had to break off the readings, so moved was I by that absolute transportation of body and soul into our native Polish plains."*

The background of these tranquil and lovely Lithuanian scenes is the war that was changing the face of Europe, for :

" The rest of the world was drowned in tears and blood ; when that man, that god of war, girt with a cloud of regiments, armed with a thousand cannons, having yoked to his car of triumph the gold with the silver eagles, flew from the Libyan plains to the sky-reaching Alps, hurling thunderbolt after thunderbolt, in the Pyramids, in Thabor, Marengo, Ulm, Austerlitz. Before him and after him ran victory and conquest. The glory of those deeds, pregnant with warriors' names, went roaring to the north, till, on the Niemen's banks, it was flung back as from a rock, by the ranks of Muscovy defending Lithuania with their walls of iron from news, terrible for Russia as the plague." (*Thaddeus*, Book I.)

Even the remote hamlets in Lithuania beat to the pulse of the events that shook the world. *Thaddeus* tells us—and amidst such scenes Mickiewicz's boyhood had been passed—how a beggar who had lost a leg or an arm would arrive at the manor, and whisper, looking round to see that no Russian soldier was near, that he was a legionary, come to die in his own land. Then the whole household, masters and servants alike, would

---

* *Correspondence of Adam Mickiewicz*, Paris, 1872. Letter of Stanislas Worcell, Nov. 7th, 1838 (Polish).

press about him, overcome by weeping, while he told them the tales they were forbidden to hear of the valour of the Polish legions, and of the victories of Napoleon. His stories were secretly repeated over the countryside. Then many a boy vanished from his home, and, escaping through the forests, swam the Niemen to the other bank where, in the Duchy of Warsaw, he might enrol himself under the Polish flags. Or a wandering friar from a foreign convent would appear at the country house, unrip his scapular, and show the war gazette that he had smuggled through. Parents then learnt for the first time after years of absence the death or glory of the son who had left them. The family went into mourning; it was guessed, but could not be told, for whom; and their obvious grief or equally obvious joy was as the war news for the district. (*Thaddeus*, Book I.)

This undercurrent of national hopes, the echo of Napoleon's trumpets, vibrate through *Thaddeus* till the end. The year 1812 is now here. The campaign, when Napoleon's armies were about to march on Russia, was greeted by the Polish nation with boundless joy, for the hour of resurrection seemed close at hand. That spring when the fields were green with unwonted promise, when the birds of passage returned early with strange clamour to their haunts in Lithuania, and the voice of war was heard in the land, was Mickiewicz's greatest memory.

" Oh, year ! " he sings in the eleventh canto of *Thaddeus*. " To this day the people call thee the year of harvest, and the soldier the year of war. To this day, the aged love to tell tales of thee, to this day song dreams of thee. Long wast thou heralded by heavenly marvel,* and preceded by low rumours among the people. With the sun of spring some strange presentiment filled Lithuanian hearts as of the end of the world ; some yearning expectation full of joy.

" Oh, spring, who saw thee in our land, memorable spring of war, and spring of harvest ! Oh, spring ! who saw thee flowering with corn and grass, brilliant in men, fertile in deed, pregnant with hope ! Still do I see thee, fair dream of a night ! Born in captivity, fettered in my swadling-bands, only one such spring have I known in my life."

Amidst this exultation and martial ardour, Thaddeus' wedding takes place. He has returned with the Polish legions for his marriage, on the advance to the Russian campaign. Side by side with the gorgeous national costume flash the accoutrements of the soldiers of the legions. Dombrowski, the hero of many a battlefield, and his fellow-generals are here. The Count, from being a weaver of fantastic fancies, has become a soldier, and sits in his Lancer uniform a guest under the roof against which he had fought. Every heart is throbbing with that patriotic rapture that, together with the glowing local colour, make the last scenes of *Thaddeus* one brilliant song of rejoicing. The banquet is carried out with all the old national traditions. The officers compete in sword-play. The patriotic Jew plays, as none other can, the *zimbala*.

" He dropped the sticks on the strings. First

* A comet that appeared in 1811.

he beat out a tune of triumph. Then, louder, he swept on the strings like a tempest of rain. It was only to test them, for soon he broke off, and he lifted the sticks on high.

" He played. Now trembled the sticks as though a fly's wing quivered over a string, giving forth a humming scarce heard. He lifted his hands ; together they fell, and he smote with both sticks.

" All at once the tune burst forth from all strings as though a Janissaries' band played on the bells, on triangles, on drums ; the Polonaise of the Third of May rings out ! * The gay notes breathe joy, make the ear drunk with joy. The girls would fain dance, the young men spring from their seats. . . .

" The master ever hurries the time, and strains at the strings. Then he struck a false chord like the hiss of a snake, like a knife grinding on glass. He plucks at the traitorous note, he confuses the tune ; tearing loud and more loud on the sullen conspirator chord that destroys the sweet sound of the strings. Then it burst with a crash, that string of ill omen."

That was how the player told in music of the conspiracy of Targowica, formed by a handful of Polish traitors, which played into the hands of Catherine II. before the second partition of Poland. He passes to the storming of Warsaw by Suvorov.

" The musician runs to the treble. He draws out a tune. The tune is confused. He casts off the treble, and runs with his sticks to the bass. Hear

---

* The day on which the liberal constitution of the Republic of Poland was passed, in 1791. This, the last great act of what remained of independent Poland, would have saved her, had her exterior enemies not been too powerful for her.

thousands of clamours ever louder, the sound of a march, and of battle, of attack, of the storming and shots, the wailing of children, and weeping of mothers. The peasant women trembled, recalling, with tears of grief, the slaughter of Praga which they knew from song and from story. They rejoiced when at last the master thundered on all the strings, then silenced their sounds as though they sank to the earth.

" Then other music. At first, light and low humming. A few slender strings sigh : "

And, after playing the songs of the legions :

" He sounded another strain, he measured the strings with his eye, and, joining his hands, he smote with both hands and both sticks. That blow was so full of art, that blow was so full of power, that the strings rang out like trumpets of brass, and like trumpets blew to the skies the famous song, the triumphal march : *Poland hath not perished. Dombrowski, march to Poland !* And all applauded and all cried out in chorus, ' March, oh, Dombrowski ! ' The player let the sticks fall from his fingers, and lifted his hands on high. . . ' General,' said he, ' long hath our Lithuania awaited thee, long as we Jews await our Messiah. Live thou and combat, oh, thou who art ours.' " (*Thaddeus*, Book XII.)

This whole passage, with its wonderful imitations of the sound of a musical instrument to which the Polish language is so peculiarly adapted, is one of the masterpieces of *Thaddeus*. My rough prose rendering can do no sort of justice to the original.

Then the company dances the Polish national

dance, the Polonaise with its intricate character figures.

" Couples followed couples, noisy and gay. They unwind ; then they turn again in a wheel, like a great snake twirling in a thousandfold scroll. The many-hued colours of the costumes of the ladies and soldiers and lords change like the flashing scales of a fish, gilt with the setting sun's rays. Whirls on fast and furious the dance, the music rings out, ring out the plaudits and toasts."

The festivity is carried on far into the night, with *Vivats* to the bridegroom and bride, to Napoleon and the leaders of the legions.

" And I ": these are the last words Mickiewicz adds to the poem : " was with the guests. I drank the wine and mead, and what I saw and heard I have gathered in this book."

The dream of the poet, who had no literary ambition, and whose thought was always with his country, was that this song of manners and tradition should penetrate to the cottage hearths of his nation, and be sung by the lips of the peasants. He had his desire. To this day *Thaddeus* remains the most beloved of poems to the Polish heart.

CHAPTER IV

THE ANONYMOUS POET OF POLAND: ZYGMUNT KRASINSKI

I

IN 1812, during the tempest of the Napoleonic wars, Zygmunt Krasinski was born into the world; he who, as the Anonymous Poet of Poland, was to stand second only to Mickiewicz in the history of his nation's literature. He was the only child of a noble house, allied by marriage to the royal family of Savoy. His father, Vincent Krasinski, played a distinguished part among the officers of the Polish legions, and Zygmunt was brought up in strong patriotic traditions. Despite the utter dissimilitude of their characters, the father and son were all their lives united by the strongest mutual affection, undestroyed even by the tragic circumstance that rose between them.

After the death of his mother, from whom he inherited his melancholy temperament and his highly strung nerves, Zygmunt led a lonely and precocious childhood in the family palace in Warsaw. The tension between the Poles and the Russian Government was then near the breaking point. The Russian Decembrist revolution took place in 1825. It was discovered that the Russian Liberals were in communication with patriotic

Polish societies. The members of the latter were, at the demand of Nicholas I., tried by the Polish Senate. The opinion of the Polish nation and of the judges was universally in favour of the accused, who were acquitted. Vincent Krasinski alone voted for their death. In 1829 the senator who had presided over the trial died. The whole of Warsaw attended the funeral as a great patriotic demonstration. All the students from the University followed the bier—with one exception, and that exception was young Krasinski. Compelled by Vincent Krasinski he, and he alone, presented himself in the lecture-hall that day, maddened with pain and rage against his father. From that moment dates the struggle, between his love for his father and his passionate devotion to his country, that was the tragedy of his life. The next day, when the class met as usual, he was mobbed as a renegade by his fellow students ; and the first to lay hands on him was one of his personal friends.

That scene branded itself for life into the soul of the proud and sensitive boy. His position in Warsaw then became impossible, and his father sent him to study at Geneva. Sad and lonely as he was, he found a warm friend in young Henry Reeve, who was completing his education in the same town. Devoured with literary ambition, Krasinski spent his time in writing essays and sketches in French and Polish prose, studying with the zest of a highly gifted youth, riding and sailing with Reeve. So passed nearly a year. He then went to Rome, and there he heard the news of the Polish Rising.

In an agony of suspense Krasinski awaited his father's summons to fight by his side. His fears were realized. The summons did not come. Already suspected by his compatriots, Vincent Krasinski now incurred their odium by taking no part in the national movement. He ended by yielding to the dictates of ambition and wounded vanity ; he went to Petersburg, in his heart still clinging to his country, and accepted favours at the hand of Nicholas I. His son's impassioned appeals were made in vain. Zygmunt now saw himself compelled, either to be at open war with his father in the sight of all the nation should he join the Rising, whither his whole heart and the traditions of his patriotic and famous house called him ; or to remain seemingly faithless to his country in the hour of her need, branded and dishonoured.

We cannot enter here into the details of the long and painful duel between father and son. At last, the latter, recoiling from the rupture that would have put Vincent Krasinski even more hopelessly in the wrong with his nation than he was already, yielded to his father's command. The anguish of mind that the boy of nineteen underwent through all this episode shattered his weak bodily frame, and laid the roots of the disease that brought him in his prime to the grave.* His tears caused the semi-blindness and threatened total loss of eyesight that from that time repeatedly recurred, cutting him off from book and pen. He never again returned of his own will to Poland, where his situation under his father's roof was

* J. Kallenbach, *Zygmunt Krasinski.* Lwów, 1904 (Polish).

unendurable. For the rest of his life, racked by mental and physical sufferings, haunted by the terror of Siberia, he wandered abroad under the supervision of the Russian Government, only going back to his native land at rare intervals for a few months, when compelled by Vincent Krasinski or by the Russian authorities. Loyalty to his father imposed upon him the concealment of his love and grief for his nation ; the acceptance of something akin to disgrace in the eyes of many of his fellow Poles. The poet who, when a brilliant boy, had longed for literary fame, now surrendered even his name. The poems and plays that he wrote, with the one intention of his country's welfare, appeared anonymously under pseudonyms, or under the names of his friends. Only his most intimate confidants knew that the Anonymous Poet was Zygmunt Krasinski. Of the many acts of self-devotion that the sons of Poland have been called upon to offer in her service, that of Zygmunt Krasinski has been one of the most bitter. He bore in silence the ruin of his life and the burden of allegiance to his father that he only laid down on his deathbed at the age of forty-seven. Unable to speak, unable to act, as he would, he was forced to hide his friendships, his opinions, his fondest predilections. He remained faithful to the two antagonistic claims that tore his heart between them ; and yet he sacrificed neither. In the part that he was driven to play, he sacrificed no principle, no person, except one —and that one was himself.*

There is nothing more in a short sketch like

* S. Tarnowski, *Zygmunt Krasinski*. Cracow, 1892 (Polish).

this to tell of his outward life. The history of Zygmunt Krasinski does not lie in exterior things, but in the battlefield of a tortured soul, and in the evolution of his mystic thought which became the highest moral teaching ever given to the Polish nation. As a poet, Krasinski is not equal to Mickiewicz. For pure artistic beauty he ranks below Slowacki. But for the nobility of the philosophy, which he spoke out of a suffering soul to a suffering country, he stands alone.

He dedicated his sad and frustrated life to Poland. He could do nothing for her except in one way, the way he chose. In his poetry and his dramas he taught her what he considered was her only means of salvation. Love, purity that spurns all evil weapons, pain borne for the redemption of humanity, is the language he incessantly speaks. Krasinski's idea was to adapt the principles of individual morality to that of a nation and of mankind.* His words were said ostensibly and mainly to a pain-stricken country; but they speak with the strongest actuality and with piercing spiritual directness to every human soul. It is this that gives Krasinski his great power, and that places him among the poets whose inspiration is a beacon light to suffering and struggling man.

Krasinski sought for the answer to the enigma of his nation's suffering until he found it. He exacted of his countrymen nothing that he himself had not given first. He did not merely watch the battle from a distance. His was the heat and burden of the field.   Those who have studied

* J. Kleiner, *History of the Thought of Zygmunt Krasinski.* Lwów, 1912 (Polish).

Krasinski's letters, which are scarcely less fine an exposition of his thought than his poetical work, are often tempted to halt astounded at the insight with which, even as a young man, he goes straight to the heart of the problems of pain and struggle. Only personal grief could have given him a like knowledge. In his youth, between the writing of *Irydion* and *Dawn*—that is, from 1836 to 1842— the sight of the fate that had befallen Poland drove him into a gulf of despair and religious doubt. He wandered for seven years in spiritual darkness, seeking always for that explanation of the wrong before his eyes which would at once save his nation and his own soul. He won to his triumph only after having, as he tells us in *Dawn*, passed through the sorrows of hell.

The masterpieces of Krasinski in which we may follow the course of his leading ideas are *The Undivine Comedy*, *Irydion*, *Dawn*, *The Psalms of the Future*, and *Resurrecturis*. As a boy of twenty-one, Krasinski wrote the sociological prose drama to which, in ironical antithesis to Dante's *Divina Commedia*, he gave the title of the *Undivine Comedy*. It is an interesting fact in Krasinski's psychology that this—the first work by which he proved his genius—is not directly national. The subject is the future class revolution to which in the poet's youth Europe appeared to be hastening. That the scene is laid in Poland we only gather from chance allusions. The characters, with the exception of the servants, are cosmopolitan rather than Polish. And yet, said Mickiewicz, who devoted several lectures in the Collège de France to its analysis, this play, with its heavy sadness, its atmosphere of ruin and approaching cataclysm, could have been written by none other than a Pole. " Its grief is not exhaled in pompous phrases ; but each word is drawn from one great mass of suffering and pain."*

The play reads as the expression of one who had gone through a great shock. Krasinski wrote it shortly after the failure of the Polish Rising, and fresh from the agony of what the Rising had brought on his personal life. There is nothing youthful in its pessimism, nothing even Byronic in its want of confidence in men. Its laconism, strangely different from the rest of Krasinski's work, is in part explained by the fact that the author was half blind when he wrote it, and had to set down his ideas on paper as briefly as he could.† The situations and characters, says Mickiewicz, live by indication rather than by development. A hint here : a half uttered phrase there ; short passages that bite into the memory like acid for their cruel curtness, their concentrated irony, their pitiless truth to one side of human nature. These things were taught by pain to the boy of twenty-one.

The *Undivine Comedy* has seemingly little connection with Krasinski's national philosophy. Indeed, at this period of his youth the poet had not discovered his spiritual bearings. Yet it foreshadows, as we shall see, some highly important elements in Krasinski's life-work. The piece of poetical prose that introduces the first part throws light on Krasinski's whole attitude to the poet's

* Adam Mickiewicz, *Les Slaves*.
† J. Kallenbach, *op. cit.*

I

calling, an attitude which, according to Mickiewicz, is Slavonic. He curses the poetry that
expresses itself only in words, and that is dead to
the deed that alone could ennoble it.

" There are stars around thy head, the waves
of the sea beneath thy feet. Before thee the rainbow runs on the waves of the sea, and cleaves
asunder the darkness. What thou beholdest is
thine. The heavens are thine. There is nought
equal to thy glory. But thou thyself, what feelest
thou ? What dost thou of thyself create ? Woe
unto thee ! Who gave thee thy base life, so false
that thou canst feign an angelic moment ere thou
wallowest in the mire, ere as a serpent thou
descendest to crawl and stifle in the slime ? Thou
sufferest, albeit thy pain shall create nought, shall
avail nought. Thou destroyest only those who
have consecrated themselves to thee, who have
become the living voices of thy glory. Blessed is
he in whom thou hast dwelt, invisible, unheard.
He will love man, and stand out as a man amidst
his brothers."

For the author of the play, said Mickiewicz,
while commenting on this description of poetry,
" poetry is not an art, not an amusement. He
has painted here the picture of the power of a soul
which flings itself entirely into its imagination,
and which believes it possesses all things, but
which is lost because it uses this gift of heaven
for its own pleasure. . . . True poetry, among the
Greeks themselves, signified nothing else except
action. What does the Polish author ask ? That
the most initiated souls, the highest, the strongest,
those that communicate with the Divinity,

should reserve all their strength to act instead of speaking."*

This preface, then, not only explains the ideals which actuated Krasinski, but it gives the clue to his conception of Henryk, the poet, the egotist, the dreamer, who is the chief character in the *Undivine Comedy*. The first part of the drama, with its subdued threatenings of the tempest that is to engulf the world, is the domestic tragedy of Henryk. The second part is the war of the classes, where Henryk is the champion of an effete and doomed aristocracy, and that culminates in a universal ruin.

Henryk has lived upon his impressions and cultivated his imagination at the expense of his heart, till he has become nothing more than a moral decadent, a poseur incapable of discerning between true and false emotion. He marries, or, as he expresses it, " descends to earthly marriage " from his dreams. " Peace to men of good will," an angel proclaims over his roof on the eve of his marriage ; and Klaczko has pointed out that Krasinski's first word to his people was this message of good will, as, in his fifth *Psalm of the Future*, it was to be well-nigh his last.† Salvation is promised to Henryk on the condition that he loves his wife : but the end of the marriage may be easily foretold. Henryk soon wearies of the loving, domestic woman, in whose soul no spark of poetry resides—except, as Klaczko observes, the poetry of a woman's devotion, a poetry truer than

---

* Adam Mickiewicz, *op. cit.*

† Julian Klaczko, *Le Poète Anonyme de la Pologne.* Revue des Deux Mondes, Jan. 1st, 1862.

any to which Henryk can lay claim. A demon maiden who stands for Henryk's old poetic ideals appears to him, tempting him from the side of his wife.

"From the day of my marriage I have slept the sleep of the torpid," says Henryk, turning with loathing from the earthly woman; "the sleep of a German manufacturer with a German wife. I have gone round after relations, doctors, shops ; and because a child is going to be born to me, I have had to think about a nurse."

When the child is born it is the same story. Henryk sits, morose and brooding, uttering short thanks as his wife unwittingly plagues him with the domesticities of the christening feast that is to be celebrated. It is with a mingling of tenderness and fidelity to fact, strange in a boy of Krasinski's years, that he paints the wronged wife ; the one sympathetic figure, for all her want of balance that ruins herself and her child, in a play which exposes on one side a rotten aristocracy, on the other savage and lawless revolutionaries. She is pierced to the heart by her husband's indifference.

"To-day, yesterday," says she, " ah, my God, and all the week, and now for three weeks, for a month, you have not said a word to me, and everybody I see tells me I look ill."

"On the contrary, I think you look well."

"It is all the same to you, because you don't look at me now. You turn away when I come in, and cover your eyes when I sit near you. Yesterday I went to confession, and remembered all my sins, and I could find nothing that could have offended you."

" You have not offended me."

" My God ! My God ! "

" I feel I ought to love you."

" You have given me the last blow with that one ' I ought.' Ah, better stand up and say, ' I do not love you.' At least I would then know all."

She starts up and takes the child from the cradle.

" Do not forsake him. Love my child, my child."

" Don't pay any attention to what I said. I often have bad moments."

" I ask you for only one word, only one promise. Say that you will always love him."

" You and him too."

He kisses her, and she clings to him. The demon maiden again enters, still the symbolization of Henryk's poetical fancies. The wife shrieks in terror. Henryk thrusts her aside, and disappears after the ghost.

The christening feast is held : a lugubrious festivity, for the father is absent, no one knows where, and the guests look curiously at the wild and pallid aspect of the mother. No softer or pitying thought can be discerned in these vapid, selfish spectators—the men who will be called to defend their order in a perishing world. The distraught mother invokes upon the infant's head, as he is baptized, her curse if he does not become a poet, so that he may gain the father's love which has been refused to her. The guests see that something unpleasant has occurred, and promptly leave the disagreeable scene. The pompous, stupid godfather—one of the most admirably drawn types in the play—utters a conventional speech over the baby's cradle, exhorting him to civic virtues, and to the love of his country. The orator himself does his best to save his own life in the end by abandoning a sinking cause.

In the course of time Henryk returns. He has been lured by the demons to the brink of a precipice, and there abandoned amidst their laughter. He comes back to find his house desolate, his wife in a lunatic asylum. The scene in the madhouse between him and the wife is handled with an extraordinary power. On all sides, above and below, ring the cries of the insane; wild and blasphemous ravings, prophetical of the convulsion of the world which will be the second part of the *Undivine Comedy*. Into these break the gentle, incoherent babblings of the wife. She tells Henryk that she has won the gift of poetry by her prayers. She falters out limping verses of her composition. She promises him that his son will be a poet. Finally, she dies in her husband's arms, happy because she breathed her last with him by her side. The characterization of Henryk is throughout true and consistent. He is shocked at the result of his conduct to his wife. He does what he can as he sits beside her in the asylum ; and the genius of Krasinski in the portrayal of a character is perhaps never more manifest than when he shows what that passionless and inefficient best of Henryk's amounts to. Outbursts of remorse or of enthusiasm can be heard from Henryk's lips at the appropriate moments ; and across them cuts a hidden voice from somewhere with the taunt or the admonition, whichever it may be : " Thou composest a drama." The fact is that Henryk has so long toyed with emotion that he himself cannot by now distinguish between genuine and false feeling. The reader instinctively suspects and remains unmoved, even in Henryk's apparently impassioned speech ; whereas every word of the wife's is spoken out of the depths of a woman's heart, carrying its sure appeal. In this lies part, at least, of the strange and subtle force of the *Undivine Comedy*.

There is one more test left in Henryk's domestic life. The angel, on the eve of his wedding, had promised him salvation if he loved his wife. The same angel, when he stood on the brink of the abyss whither the demon had led him, promised him salvation if he returned and loved his son. There remains, then, the child, the strange, mournful child who sees visions and talks to his dead mother. He is said to be the reminiscence of Krasinski's own shadowed childhood. His blindness is described with the psychology of intimacy, for while Krasinski wrote the play he was nearly blind himself. The son's hallucinations are the embodiment before his father's eyes of the latter's punishment, of the spirit of poetry in its destructive form. The child is the type of a soul that is too weak to cope with a difficult world, whose only refuge is in dreams, and whose death is as unnecessary as his life had been futile.*

Whatever Henryk's egoism, Krasinski was too great an artist to paint him without affection for an only son.† His knowledge of human nature rather chose to represent the decadent husband, who wearied of an uninteresting and domestic wife, as a selfish but not indifferent father of a son

* J. Klaczko, *op. cit.*   † J. Kleiner, *op. cit.*

who was, after all, part of himself. The child is doomed by the physician to incurable blindness. " Thy son is a poet," calls the unknown voice. " What more couldst thou desire ? " But for once Henryk's grief rings true. There is no pose in his cry : " Is there no, no hope ? "

He wanders in the mountains. What is left to him ? His family happiness, through his doing, is shattered. His only child, the inheritor of his house, is blind, and more or less mad. He has tried philosophy, and all in vain. The society in which he has been brought up is dissolving. He has known every feeling " by name, and there is no faith, hope or love left in me." He has, indeed, loved his son, but with the love of self that could not save him. Then the demon again appears to him, this time under the form of an eagle representing ambition ; and henceforth Henryk is dominated by the lust of power.

Now begins the second part of the *Undivine Comedy*. The revolution is let loose upon the world. The remnants of the aristocracy, wretched, boneless specimens, are making their last stand in the fortress of the Trinity. Once, in the long past, as we know from a poem of Krasinski's which, written after the *Undivine Comedy*, was intended to be its introduction, and which remains unfinished, Henryk had had his dreams of a people's liberties. Now, not from conviction, for he is not convinced, not from enthusiasm to a cause, for his heart is too worn out to harbour enthusiasm, but from the desire to play the part of a leader of men and to go out with all eyes upon him, he is the champion and the commander of the nobles.

Opposed to him is Pancracy, the head of the revolutionaries. No softening element has ever entered Pancracy's life. Nameless, he has grown up in misery, hunger, toil. He will stop short of nothing. His camp is a shambles, given up to orgies of bloodshed and licence, described in scenes that are in part founded on the excesses of the French revolution, and in part on certain of the tenets of Saint-Simonism. That Krasinski had no want of sympathy with the oppressed classes is obvious, from the pathos which he put into the complaints of the men and women whose whole existence had been a round of treadmill labour, unsweetened by any joy. But he saw no hope for the future either in the effete ruling class, or in a revolution where violence was the mistress. Where love is not and where the heart is absent there can be no victory, according to Krasinski. So he presents both aristocrat and democrat with a like cold severity. So he figures Pancracy as having his moments of wavering, even as Henryk has. He can convince others, but not himself. Should he be able to win Henryk over his confidence will be assured, and the one impediment to his triumph will be removed. And so the two meet secretly in Henryk's castle.

In this scene, Henryk's self-dramatization comes out with startling clearness. His family escutcheons hang on the walls about him. He summons now the shades of his ancestors, now the God of his fathers, to assist him in the interview. Pious sentiments flow from his lips. He has assumed the attitude of the defender of Christianity.

Religion is his aristocratic heritage—and it counts for nothing else in his life.

Pancracy enters.

" I greet Count Henryk. That word 'Count' sticks in my throat. If I am not mistaken, these red and blue badges are called coats of arms in the language of the dead. There are ever fewer of such little dots on the face of the earth."

Henryk : " With the help of God you will soon see thousands of them."

Pancracy : " There is my old nobility. Always sure of themselves. Haughty, obstinate, flourishing with hope, and without a farthing, without a weapon, without soldiers, believing, or pretending they believe, in God ; for it would be difficult to believe in themselves ! "

Henryk : " Atheism is an ancient formula, and I expected something new from you."

Pancracy : " I have a stronger, a mightier faith than yours. The groans torn by despair and pain from thousands of thousands, the hunger of workmen, the misery of peasants, the shame of their wives and daughters. That is my faith and my God for to-day."

Henryk : " I have placed my strength in the God Who gave the government to my fathers."

Pancracy : " And all your life you have been the plaything of the devil. As for the rest, I leave this discussion to theologians, if some pedant of the trade still exists in the country. To business ! I came here because I wanted to know you, and, in the second place, to save you."

He attempts to move Henryk. The latter entrenches himself behind his sworn oath.

" Knightly honour has come upon the scene,"
sneers Pancracy. " That is a faded rag on the
banner of humanity. Oh, I know you. You ally
yourself with the dying because you want to
deceive yourself, because you want to believe still
in caste, in the bones of your great-grandmothers,
in the word *my country* ; but in the bottom of
your heart you know that the punishment is
owing to your brethren, and, after the punishment, oblivion."

Henryk : " And what else is there for you and
yours ? "

Pancracy : " Victory and life. I only recognize
one law. That law is your destruction, and through
my lips it cries : ' Decrepit worms, full of food
and drink, yield to the young, the hungry and the
strong.' "

Then Pancracy paints the golden age which the
revolution will bring about. He speaks alike to the
nobler dreams that had been Henryk's in his
youth and to the poseur's weakest side :

" If you know how to reach immortality, if you
love truth and have sought it sincerely, if you are
a man in the pattern of humanity and not of
nursery rhymes, do not throw away this moment
of salvation. If you are what you once seemed to
be, rise up and follow me."

For the moment, Henryk wavers. Pancracy's
words sound to his ear as the murmuring of the
" dead sea-shell " of his lost days. Even his spent
heart experiences a stab at the recollection of the
ideals that had gone from him. Meanwhile Pancracy
looks on with the sarcastic comment—a sufficient
index that his appeal to Henryk was not that of a

deeply felt truth : " I have touched the nerve of poetry."

But neither can win over the other. The *Undivine Comedy* is the drama of negation. No conversion to an opposing side can enter within its scope.[*]

Driven by hunger and panic, Henryk's adherents, feeble to the end, drop away from his side. The avenging, innocent witness, against whom the husband and father can have no redress, leads Henryk into the vaults of the castle, and recounts to him the vision he sees of his father's damnation. Voices of invisible spirits wail ; " Because thou hast loved nought save thyself, because thou hast worshipped nought save thyself, thou art damned —damned for all eternity." All hope is gone. The enemies are at the gate. The son is slain by a chance shot at his father's feet ; but Henryk can still exult that his own life will go down in a blaze of glory. The fortress is captured. Henryk stands poised for a moment in the sight of his foes on the ramparts above the precipice. " Poetry, be thou cursed by me, as I shall be cursed for all eternity," is his last cry ; and, with hands outstretched as a swimmer about to plunge, he leaps down into the darkness.

The victory, then, is with Pancracy. One by one, he sweeps off the miserable survivors of the old order to the death, which they face with the same want of fortitude that characterized their lives. He stands, as Henryk stood, on the ramparts. Wherever his gaze rests he beholds the new world he has created. Then, on a sudden, he cries aloud

[*] St. Tarnowski, *Zygmunt Krasinski.*

to his companion. For, above the cloud on fire
with the light of the setting sun, appears to him,
and him alone, a sign of terror. He sees One Who
rises :

" As a pillar of snow-white brilliance above
the precipices. Both hands lean on the cross as the
avenger's on his sword. Of wreathed thunderbolts
is the crown of thorns. From the lightning of
that glance he must die who lives. Put thy hands
on my eyes. Smother my eyeballs with your fists.
Part me from that look that shatters me to dust.
Thy hands are transparent as water, transparent
as glass, transparent as air. I see still ! Give me if
only a crumb of darkness ! Darkness—darkness !
Galilaee, vicisti ! "

He falls dead, and the *Undivine Comedy* ends.

What remains ? Nothing except a ruined world,
where every living thing has gone down in the
waters of destruction and desolation. Klaczko has
said that the *Undivine Comedy* is " a farewell
rather than a greeting addressed by the poet to
humanitarian inspirations, a strong protest against
the fatal illusion of the age which believes it can
regenerate humanity without having first regen-
erated the man, and establish universal right
without having first strengthened the individual
in his duties."* It is this moral, deep down beneath the surface, and the dramatic conclusion,
told in a few scathing sentences, that redeem the
Undivine Comedy from being an expression of
unrelieved pessimism, and that give the link without
which Krasinski's subsequent work might seem
a far cry from the play of his youth. He saw

* J. Klaczko, *op. cit.*

a world where two opposing forces disputed for its mastery. He saw, albeit he does not speak in the *Undivine Comedy* with that certainty of his maturer years which suffering taught him, still he saw that final triumph lay with neither, but beyond.*

The *Undivine Comedy* resembles nothing that Krasinski ever wrote again. Not only does its curious terseness give it a place apart in the production of a poet, whose literary sin is a tendency to over ornamentation and elaboration ; but its unbroken dreariness, its pessimism, are not characteristic of Krasinski as a writer. Devoured by sadness all his life, never expecting and never finding personal happiness, he yet looked with confidence to the resurrection of his nation ; and, deep as are the accents of sorrow that breathe through his poetry, the keynote of that poetry is hope.†

II

The idea of *Irydion* came to Krasinski before that of the *Undivine Comedy* ; but the latter was finished first. During the years that the poet was writing *Irydion* his life was racked with passion, and he could not complete it till 1836.

In 1830, in the days preceding the Rising, he wandered about the Coliseum, then the most

* Adam Mickiewicz, *Les Slaves.*

† Lord Lytton's *Orval* is a sort of paraphrase of Krasinski's *Undivine Comedy*. Taken from a French rendering, it is in no sense a translation, but rather a version of Krasinski's story with scarcely any resemblance to the Polish original.

I may add that I am preparing a translation of the *Undivine Comedy* direct from the Polish.

poetical of ruins, dreaming by moonlight. His dreams slowly took shape in the form of the Greek who plotted in Rome for the overthrow of the empire that had enslaved his country, and who was given his sentence at the foot of the cross in the Flavian amphitheatre. The first time that Krasinski returned to Poland, after he had left it as a boy, was in 1832. He stayed a few weeks in his home ; and was then obliged by his father to spend the winter with him in Petersburg. That winter was one of Krasinski's dreariest remembrances. He was overcome with grief at the fate of Poland, lonely and desolate of soul in the capital of Russia, parted from all his friends with whom—Polish exiles as they were—he might not correspond. To Reeve alone could he write, albeit with strict reserve, because the letters were read by the censor, and also because the condition of his eyes frequently compelled him to dictate his correspondence. More or less blind, he could do nothing but remain all the winter shut up in one room, with no occupation or distraction except his father's visits and his own meditations, and that one painful and perilous audience with Nicholas I., which he has told under an allegorical form in his *Temptation*. Under these circumstances, he evolved the conception of *Irydion*, his Thought, as he always called it. The Pole in Petersburg put his feelings into the son of Hellas who trod the streets of Rome with rage in his heart. Yet the teaching of *Irydion* is that hatred for the oppressor will compass the destruction of the nation that employs it, and that love, and only love, is the constructive force of a downtrodden people.

Unable for his father's sake to speak openly, unable for his own sake to do so in days when frank language was liable to send writer, as well as reader, to Siberia, Krasinski couched his meaning under a symbolism where he who ran might read.

The morals that Krasinski urges upon his countrymen are invariably forgiveness and love ; but his confidences to his intimate friends lay bare the nature of the battle that he fought against himself. His heart, as a young man, was swept by a storm of hatred for those who had brought misery upon his nation. He wrote—in 1831—to Henry Reeve :

" You, a free man, a man born free, you cannot understand the feelings of a man whose ancestors were as free as you, but who is himself an oppressed slave. You have never seen a young and beautiful woman weeping hot tears for the loss of her honour, torn from her by the brutality of a conqueror. You have never heard the chains quivering around the arms of your compatriots. In the night, the sounds of lamentations have not made you start from your sleep, you have not risen on your pillow, you have not listened half asleep to the wheels jolting on the pavement, the wheels of the cart that carried your relation, your friend, to the snows of Siberia. You have not been forced to hear a hard, rough language thrust on a people who did not understand it. You have not caught a glimpse of the haggard faces of your brothers through the grating of a prison. Round the winter hearth, you have never been told how such a one disappeared, how another was condemned, how this village was burnt, that town sacked, and all Praga drowned in the blood of its inhabitants, children flung palpitating on the frozen, stiff breasts of their mothers. . . You have not followed on the map the desolation of your country, till it was at last overwhelmed under the weight of the oppressors. To you everything has spoken of peace, happiness, forgetfulness. That is why hatred appears so hideous to you. Hatred was the companion of my childhood. I hated with all the strength of my little heart before I loved either a woman or friend. It is an element which has mingled with my nature and which has become a part of my being."*

To a Polish friend, better able than the prosperous young Englishman to understand the strength of the temptation, Krasinski confided that his sympathies were with Irydion, the hater and the avenger, and that only logic and necessity led him to the conclusion of love triumphant that makes the moral grandeur of the play. "What is, is," he added. " It is not our caprices that rule the world, but the mind of God."† *Irydion* represents the victory of Krasinski's higher self, a life-giving truth spoken from the anguish of one Pole to the anguish of thousands of Poles.

The length of the drama, the elaboration of the style, the wealth of detail that, indeed, at times somewhat overlays the main purpose, are in

* *Correspondance de Sigismond Krasinski et de Henry Reeve,* Paris, 1902. Letter of Krasinski to Reeve, Nov. 18, 1831.
† *Letters of Zygmunt Krasinski.* Vol. I, To Constantine Gaszynski, June 6, 1837.

K

strong contrast with the *Undivine Comedy*. *Irydion*
glows with the colour and pageantry of Imperial
Rome. It was Krasinski's mental refuge to picture
the blue skies of the south, as he thought out
Irydion during the long winter in a snow-bound
city, where all that his half-blind eyes could see
from his window were white roofs and a gray pall
of clouds.*

Irydion is the son of Amphilochus the Greek
and of a Scandinavian priestess. The touch of
northern blood is required in order to give Krasinski's " Thought " its mystic link with the north,
and also as foretelling the direction from which
Rome's fall was to come upon her. The scene is
laid in the reign of Heliogabalus. Both of Irydion's
parents are dead when the drama, which is written
in prose, begins. He and his sister, Elsinoe, are
alone, under the tutelage of a majestic and mysterious old man, called Masinissa, in reality,
Mephistopheles. Nursed in hatred of Rome,
Irydion has been brought up with the one idea of
compassing, not his nation's resurrection, but the
ruin of her conqueror. To that end he is stealthily
proceeding. Every weapon, however ignoble,
suits his purpose if only it can bring about the
desired result. On all sides he sows treachery,
destruction, disgrace—for the sake of finally
destroying Rome.

His master move is to sacrifice his sister's honour
to Heliogabalus, and, through her, to play on the
fears and caprices of the half-childish emperor,
till the latter becomes a tool in the Greek's hands.
The farewell of Irydion and Elsinoe on the evening

* J. Kallenbach, *op. cit.*

when the imperial slaves are coming to fetch her away is the first scene of the drama. Here, as in the madhouse episode in the *Undivine Comedy*, Krasinski handles a terrible situation with artistic power and restraint. The beautiful child, for she is little more, throws herself weeping on the mercy of her brother.

" Thou knowest," is his reply, " that thou art no more my sister, thou art not the golden-haired Elsinoe, the hope of thy father's house, the darling of my heart. Thou art the victim appointed for the suffering of many and for the shame of thy fathers."

Elsinoe : " Yea. You all have taught me this from childhood, and I am ready. But still not to-day, not to-morrow—a little later, when I have gathered strength, when I have heard more of Masinissa's teaching and thy commands, when I have drunk to the bottom of the chalice of your poison."

Irydion : " Thou art chosen. We needs must hasten on the road we tread."

Elsinoe : " Remember when we played on the grass-plots of Chiara, I loved thee so. Oh, have mercy on me ! "

Irydion : " Woman, thou temptest me to pity in vain, in vain."

Elsinoe : " Why so many prayers and tears ? It was possible in times of old to save oneself by death from men and gods. See, thy dagger flashes there, Irydion. Let us hasten annihilation for ourselves, Irydion."

Irydion : " Thou blasphemest against thy father's thought. Of old the life of one man sufficed for the salvation of nations. To-day the times are otherwise. To-day the sacrifice must be of honour." *He clasps her in his arms.* "To-day thou shalt be wreathed with roses, decked with smiles. Oh, unhappy child, lay here thy doomed head. For the last time in thy father's house thy brother presses thee to his bosom. Take thy farewell of me in all the beauty of thy maiden freshness. Never again shall I behold thee young— never, never again."

Then he, too, fails at the thought of what he is doing. He cries to Masinissa for support. His hesitation, Elsinoe's prayers and tears, all alike die at the entrance of the old man. Adorned as a bride, weeping and swooning, the girl is carried off by the slaves of Heliogabalus ; but Irydion's end is gained. He, and Elsinoe acting under his orders, assume entire dominion over the young emperor, the mad, childish degenerate whose personality stands out in vivid colours in Krasinski's drama. Irydion soon convinces him that he, the Greek, is his only friend, and that no safety will be his till he abandons the city and retires to build up another in the east. In the meanwhile, the traitor tampers with the Praetorians, and lures the barbarians and gladiators to his side. They only wait Irydion's signal to fall upon Rome ; but Irydion is not ready yet. He believes that Rome cannot be destroyed unless he wins the adhesion of the Christians, and they, he knows, will not consent to fight against their persecutors whom their Founder bade them forgive. Masinissa persuades him to go down into the catacombs, to feign the profession of Christianity and receive baptism and then, seemingly as a fervent neophyte, by all the craft in his power to sow dissension among the Christians, and convince the more restless and impetuous that it is their duty to take up arms. Irydion is baptized by the name of Hieronimus. He attempts to work his will with the Christians. But the task is a difficult one. Masinissa counsels him to dupe some Christian virgin, and to play upon her religious exaltation till it turns into love for him. Then, when she is his, victory will follow. For once, Irydion shrinks. He has in his mind Cornelia, the pure and beautiful maiden, vowed to Christ, who has talked to him of his soul.

"Must all that is holy and dear to others be ever a sacrilege for me? Who made me miserable and vile? She, who is the murderess of all my moments, whose name is Rome."

"There is another Rome," answers Masinissa, "that cannot perish. Not on seven hills, but on millions of stars have her feet rested." Against that Rome Irydion must swear eternal enmity. And Irydion, calling on "unhappy Hellas," consents for love of her to destroy another's joy, "to tear hope away from one who hoped."

Masinissa is Satan. Krasinski's conception of a Mephistopheles is unusual. He is grand, majestic, and, save in certain moments when he speaks or acts openly as the minister of hatred, passionless. His attitude with Irydion is less that of a tempter than of a conspirator on equal terms. He incites or encourages Irydion to vile deeds, such as the sacrifice of the two women in the play; but it is in the name of a sacred cause that he does so, for

the love of Hellas. He will ruin souls by his appeal, not to their baser, but to their higher, desires.*
Krasinski's idea in the presentment of this Mephistopheles is that he is the satan of the world's policy ; the evil spirit of humanity that thrusts governments and peoples back from the road of spiritual progress, that would warp a nation's love to destroy her by that love itself.†

Irydion has already brought disunion and confusion where before all was brotherly charity and steadfast purpose. He has set the young men among the Christians on fire for battle in the name of God. The old men, headed by the Pope, Victor, seek to hold them back, appalled at the thought of taking the blood of their persecutors. If only Cornelia, who is venerated as a saint by her fellow-believers, will persuade them to listen to Irydion, his cause is won. He, therefore, sets himself to deceive her by every wile of diabolical craft that his cunning can suggest, into which against his will the touch of human passion on his side now and again steals. They stand together alone in the bowels of the earth, among the corridors of the dead stretching as far as eye can reach. The maiden, in whose portrayal there is the tenderness of touch, the strange, elusive charm peculiar to Krasinski's women, trembles for Irydion's soul. The Greek, dark and gloomy, watches her as with the eyes of a snake on the bird he is ensnaring. She entreats him to desist from his thirst for bloodshed that she can only look upon as sin.

* J. Kleiner, *History of the Thought of Zygmunt Krasinski.*
† St. Tarnowski, *Zygmunt Krasinski.*

" Alas ! Art thou the same with whom I knelt in the cemetery of Eufemia, to whom I taught my prayer ? Hieronimus, is this thou ? I have prayed so much, I have done such hard penance for so many days and nights."

Irydion : " And thou shalt reach heaven. Who could doubt it ? "

Cornelia : " Oh, it was not for myself, not for myself."

Irydion : " Then for whom ? "

Cornelia : " One of my brothers."

Terrified at the frenzy, whether real or feigned, of a jealous lover which she in her innocence takes for a delirium she does not understand, she confesses that this brother was he. Little by little, Irydion lets sink into her ear the idea that she is dishonouring her God, Who is his God too, by not desiring the warfare for His glory that Irydion desires.

" Oh, Lord, for mercy, mercy on him do I call," pleads Cornelia. " Thou wilt not suffer him to be lost before my eyes. Ah ! what am I saying ? Where am I ? Surely, oh, Lord, I have vowed my whole heart to Thee. How dark and gloomy is it here ! For the first time terror of the dead falls on me."

Irydion : " Lean on me."

Gradually the hints of the tempter do their work. Trouble and doubt enter the soul of the innocent girl. Irydion weaves the story of the vow to revenge himself on Rome, to which his father trained him, with the vision of Christ's kingdom triumphing, till she can no longer distinguish issues. She only knows that a mortal face has fastened itself into her thoughts where Christ alone reigned before ; " and as a prophet, a saint, an archangel, he stands before me and speaks, and I listen to him, oh, Lord, and I would fain die. Have mercy on me ! "

She strives to defend him against his temptation to vengeance, herself against the unknown forces that are carrying her away. Overcome with detestation of the deed he is about to do, Irydion bids her leave him. No, she will not leave him to his sin. She implores him to kneel and pray by her side.

" You are my witness, bones of the dead," murmurs he, " and thou, mother earth, I would fain have spared her, and her only."

He hears the voice of Simeon, the leader of the Christian youths whom he has gained over, calling him to the battle. Then he tears the veil from Cornelia's head, and implants his kisses on her forehead. With the cry that she is damned with him for ever, she swoons. She wakes, mad, to find Irydion standing by her. He tells her he is Christ, come to claim His victory with arms. His end is secured. Cornelia runs frenzied through the catacombs, crying out : " To arms ! "

All is now clamour and discord. Victor tries in vain to restrain Simeon's band. Irydion, surrounded by his barbarians, urges them forward by all that is sacred to them, and which he pretends is equally sacred to himself. Cornelia's wild cries " To arms !" ring above the tumult, and, coming from the lips of the saint of the catacombs, seem a summons from heaven. Masinissa, at this moment appearing openly as the demon, rises in the midst of columns of fire, exulting in the ravages that have been, and will be, wrought in the souls of the followers of Christ.

" Faith, hope and love ! Trinity, which wast to last for ever, I have torn Thee to shreds in the hearts of the most beloved children of Thy benediction ! In Thy name they shall slay and burn. In Thy name they shall oppress. Thou shalt be crucified alike in their wisdom and their ignorance, alike in the sleepy humility of their prayers and in the blasphemies of their pride."

And now the moment for which Irydion has schemed so long is close at hand. Irydion wrings from the terror-stricken emperor his command over the Praetorians. Alexander Severus is marching on Rome ; and the avenger has sworn his death no less than that of Heliogabalus, with an equal certainty that neither of them must live to prolong the life of Rome. Elsinoe, throwing herself into her brother's arms, entreats him :

" Let those eyes die beneath which I withered. Let the arms which crawled about my neck fall as two worn-out vipers. Let the lips which first touched mine perish in ashes."

Irydion : " On the same heap and at the same moment, both he and Severus."

Elsinoe : " Not so, not so. Let me finish my last desire. Spare Alexander on the field of battle. He with one look calmed my despair. He alone guessed. Ah, why hast thou turned thy face away from me ? "

Irydion : " He is the only one who is now tearing Rome from the clasp of my hatred."

Elsinoe : " Then once more press thy sister to

thy bosom. Feelest thou how this heart throbs ?
Ere thou returnest, it will have broken, son of
Amphilochus ! But remember Elsinoe desired no
blood of thee. Let live all, all—even he, the
Syrian, the abominated—let him live."

Voices outside the palace : "Forward, in the
name of the Fortune of Irydion the Greek."

Irydion : "Away with untimely mourning,
when Nemesis already holds the crown of vengeance for us in each hand. Victory descends into
my soul. In those clashings of arms, in those shouts,
leaps my life, and must thou die ? Rather be
happy and proud. What thy father invoked, what
long ages have asked of the gods with tears,
approaches as the thunderbolt."

Voices : "Irydion, Irydion ! "

Irydion : "Farewell."

Elsinoe : "Go. Be thou happy and mighty ;
and if ever thou shalt sail on the Acgean waters
cast a handful of my ashes on Chiara's banks."

They part for ever. When Alexander Severus'
troops rush into the palace. Heliogabalus is holding to his lips the cup of poison he dares not
drink, and is despatched by the soldiers. Elsinoe,
garbed in imperial robes, sits calmly waiting. As
the curtains of her apartment are torn aside, she
pierces her heart with a dagger, preferring death
rather than the love that might be hers of the
saviour of Rome, Alexander Severus.

But we anticipate. Alexander is not victorious
yet. The night that Irydion hails as the last night
of Rome is here. His armies are awaiting his
signal. Masinissa is at his side. With wild fury
Irydion exults in the thought that, before the

morning is upon them, Rome shall be in flames—
if, and upon this condition all depends, the
Christian auxiliaries join him. They delay. They
are singing their hymns, says Masinissa sardon-
ically. A messenger from Simeon summons Irydion.
He hastens to the catacombs. He finds Victor and
the priests on the altar steps, Simeon and his
youths in arms, panting for the fray, Cornelia
still uttering her frenzied war-cry. Irydion bursts
upon this assembly. He calls to Cornelia as to his
beloved ; but pitted against him is Victor who
stands forth and, in the presence of all, exorcises
Cornelia. She returns to herself. She bears witness
that she and her fellow Christians have been
duped by an evil spirit that has possessed her and
spoken through her lips. In vain Irydion, with
one despairing effort, calls to her in the language
of love for the last time. She turns to him without
fear and with forgiveness. " Hieronimus, I
pardon thee. Hieronimus, pray to Christ " ; and
so she dies, breathing the fragrance of the flowers
of Paradise.

Her testimony turns the Christians, loathing
and horror-stricken, from him whom they now
see in his true colours. The maddened Irydion
tears the cross he wears from his armour and,
dashing it to the ground, departs, doomed, as he
well knows, to failure. In the catacombs the
avenger has been brought up against the only
life-giving element in Rome. With that force
behind him, he can conquer. With it against
him, he can do nothing. All that is now left to
him is to fight a losing battle "more like a demon
than a mortal man." The envoy of Alexander

Severus brings him overtures of peace. He rejects them with a certain noble contempt. His nation has loved, and lived on, an idea. What has she to do with an empire that has maintained herself by blood and by the tears of the conquered ?

So Irydion fights on ; but ever and again his sword falters in his hand and he turns pale, for he hears Cornelia calling to him in the name of Christ. He is defeated, and abandoned by all. He steps on Elsinoe's funeral pyre and prepares to perish in the flames. Masinissa descends, and carries him away to a mountain top. In the distance lies Rome. The enemy of Irydion's race stands out on her hills, her marbles flashing in the sun, proud and invincible.

" Oh, thou whom I loved for thy sorrows, wast thou but a shade ? " What now remains to Irydion ? The voice of the Christian maiden, whom he sacrificed at Masinissa's bidding, wails in his ear. He sees the cross at which she prayed. If her God were indeed a God above all gods, it is on Him that he would now call.

" Our Father, Who art in heaven," sneers Masinissa, " give long days to Rome. Save those who through all time have oppressed my native land."

" Nay," is Irydion's reply. " Our Father Who art in heaven, love Hellas as I have loved her." He then adjures Masinissa to tell him if Christ is indeed the " Lord of heaven and earth." Masinissa confesses Him, but as his immortal enemy. He bids Irydion gaze at the " city of his hatred." Who shall tear it from the hands of Irydion's northern brothers when their hordes overwhelm Italy? The Nazarene. But Irydion must not despair. A day will come when " on the Forum only dust shall remain, in the Circus only ruins, on the Capitol only shame." That day is so distant that Masinissa himself can hardly foresee it; but, if Irydion will consent to renounce Christ for ever, Masinissa will cast him into a slumber of centuries till he awakes to behold the ruin of Rome. A voice once known to Irydion cries in anguish and entreaty: but he agrees to the bond, and sinks into a deep sleep in a cavern in the hills outside Rome.

Here the dramatic form of *Irydion* ends, and the conclusion is told in an epilogue.

The ages roll over Irydion's head.

" Oh, my Thought "—the poet thus addressing Irydion—" thou hast lasted out the centuries ! Thou didst slumber in the day of Alaric and in the day of the mighty Attila. Neither the ring of the imperial crown on the rough brow of Charlemagne, nor Rienzi, the tribune of the people, woke thee—and the consecrated lords of the Vatican one after the other passed before thee, as shades before a shade. But to-day thou shalt arise, oh, my Thought ! "

He rises in the strength of his youth at the appointed hour—the days of Krasinski.

" Thou didst stand in the Roman Campagna. She hath nought with which to hide her shame before thy gaze. The aqueducts running to the city, finding no city, have halted. The stones fallen from them lie in graveyard heaps.

" The son of the ages saw and rejoiced in the justice of his vengeance. Each ruin, and the plains, widowed of amphitheatres, and the hills, orphaned of temples, were his recompense."

He passes on to Rome, guided by Masinissa. He beholds the ruins of the Baths of Caracalla, the Appian way laid waste, the Forum a mass of fragments. He halts in the Coliseum. As he stands in the arena, surrounded by the gaping walls about which festoons of greenery cling, some strange emotion stirs within the Greek. He looks upon the cross that stands there—as it stood in Krasinski's youth—with some far off recollection of a maiden's face; and he knows that now he no longer desires war with the cross, for it seems to him as though that cross is " weary as he, sorrowing as once Hellas sorrowed—and holy for evermore."

Then begins in the Coliseum, at the foot of the cross, the judgment upon Irydion's soul—a scene that had developed in Krasinski's heart since he had wandered, when little more than a boy, about the ruin in the moonlight. The amphitheatre resounds with the sighs of the martyrs who shed their blood there, with the wailing of the angels above. Below the cross stands Irydion with prayerless lips. Masinissa claims the damned soul for his own. In the light of the moon shines a beautiful face, angelic wings flash, as Cornelia battles for the salvation of him who wronged her. " Immortal Enemy," is the cry of Masinissa, " he is mine, for he lived in revenge, and he hated Rome." " Oh, Lord, he is mine," rings the cry of Cornelia, " for he loved Greece."

The plea of love prevails, as in the scheme of *Irydion* it must prevail. Irydion had hated ; but, unlike Henryk of the *Undivine Comedy*, who was damned because he had loved nothing, Irydion had loved Greece. He had sinned, but sinned because he had loved. He is, therefore, saved, but not without a long expiation. He who had worked in hatred, and whose work had therefore resulted only in its own destruction, is now sent to a labour of love for a fallen country that will surely save both him and her. In the sentence pronounced by heaven upon Irydion—Krasinski's mystic and national Thought—the poet throws off, in part, the allegory, and speaks more plainly to his brother Poles. Irydion is bidden :

" 'Go to the north in the name of Christ. Go and halt not till thou standest in the land of graves and crosses. Thou shalt know it by the silence of men and the sadness of little children, by the ruined huts of the poor and the destroyed palaces of the exiles. Thou shalt know it by the sighs of My angels, flying over it by night.'

" 'Go and dwell among the brothers that I give thee. There, is thy second trial. For the second time thou shalt behold thy love trans-pierced, dying—and the sorrows of thousands shall be born in thy one heart.'

" 'Go and trust in My name. Ask not for thy glory, but for the good of those whom I entrust to thee. And, after long martyrdom, I will give ye what I gave My angels—happiness—and what I promised to mankind on the heights of Golgotha —freedom.'

" ' Go and act. Although thy heart shall faint in thy bosom, although thou shalt doubt thy brethren although thou shouldst despair of Me Myself, act ever and without rest. And thou shalt rise, not from sleep as erst, but from the work of ages—and thou shalt be the free son of heaven.'

"And the sun rose above the ruins of Rome. And there was none whom I might tell where were the traces of my Thought—but I know that it lasts and lives."

Irydion is the confession of one who knew the onslaughts of despair and hatred, and who overcame them, both for himself and his nation, by holding fast to the principles of an unflinching national morality. Criticising his drama from the ethical standpoint, which was the only aspect under which Krasinski ever spoke of his work in his correspondence with his friends, the poet said :

"To prove its truth, the author might call upon the shades of the dead and the tears of the living. He might ask many a one : ' Didst thou not feel this, didst thou not dream thus ? ' And many a one would answer : ' It is so.' Not many a one, but a whole nation."*

III

The development of Krasinski's thought was not, as might have been imagined, a triumphal progress from *Irydion* onwards. After the completion of the latter, darkness and confusion swept down upon the poet. From his own testimony in the opening lines to *Dawn*, we know that it was his grief for his country that shook both his

* *Letters of Zygmunt Krasinski.* Vol. I. To Constantine Gaszynski, June 6, 1837.

religious and national faith, always closely inter-
woven in Krasinski's soul. At this time he wrote
but little, and nothing that was worthy of his
genius, chiefly obscure allegories in poetic prose,
overladen with excessive imagery, tinged here
and there with pantheism, and indicative of the
spiritual perplexity in which he dwelt. Yet
through *The Temptation*, *The Summer Night*,
through the strange, nightmare visions of the
Three Thoughts, there runs the one thread that
nothing could ever destroy or weaken in Krasinski's life, which was at once his ruling passion
and the chief source of all his suffering : devotion
to Poland. They are the cry of one bewildered
with pain, unable to see with certainty his nation's
deliverance.

Curiously enough, Krasinski, the dreamer, the
poet, the mystic, was above all things a logician.
His national philosophy must be founded on a
rational system, it must convince his mind no less
than his heart, before it could satisfy him. Through
the years of mental suffering that stretched between the writing of *Irydion* and *Dawn*, he was
seeking a theory that would give the key to the
mystery of Poland's tragedy, provide her with a
hope, proclaim a vocation for her in the future.
Every philosophical development, every political
event, was significant in this connection alone. At
last, he found what his soul had asked. *Dawn* is
the hymn of his spiritual and patriotic victory.

His idea may be thus roughly summarized.
The signs of the times that immediately preceded
the birth of Christ—religious doubt, moral decadence, strange faiths—are almost identical with

L

those of Krasinski's age. The conquests of Julius Cæsar paved the way for the coming of Christ by obliterating the frontiers between nations. In the nineteenth century we have the Napoleonic conquests ; and these, in their turn, prepared the world for Christ's second and spiritual advent. Not again in our flesh. But as He christianized the individual, so now He will christianize governments, and harmonize the relations between them and their subjects, between nation and nation. As long as the dismemberment of Poland, that crime against law and right, is permitted to be an established fact, so long is Christ's intention violated. Her restoration will be the herald of the transfiguration of the political sphere into the religious sphere, an earnest of the higher epoch of the world's history.

Thus Krasinski in his prose introduction to *Dawn*.* And hence the mystic rapture with which he can announce to his people that Poland's death leads to her resurrection, her shame to the glorious re-birth of the human race.

" Hodie scietis quia veniet Dominus et salvabit nos et mane videbitis gloriam ejus." These words from the office of his Church for Christmas Eve, Krasinski places at the head of the poem that is one of the noblest expressions in literature of a nation's suffering and a nation's hope.

As Dante's *Divina Commedia* is the spiritual apotheosis of a woman, so *Dawn* is the idealization of her whom Krasinski etherealized as his Beatrice, and who likewise inspired Poland's greatest

* See Chapter II.

musician—Delphina Potocka.* In the lines which open *Dawn* the poet sings how he was driven forth from the land of his fathers to tread strange soil, hearing from afar the triumphal cries of those who had laid his country low.

" Like Dante, during life, I passed through hell.

" At first, I trusted that the pitying God, Who is proud to the proud, to the faithful full of faith ; at first, I trusted after days but few He would send avenging angels from above, and burst that grave that stands before the world. But the days passed by, and passed away the years. In vain dawn struggled with the blinded strength of night. No sun arose above the grave of saints ; and ever more abased did this earth of ours become. Then sank my soul into that chaos of doubt, where all light is changed into eternal night : and, from all the circle of those lived out days, one inscription standeth : *There is no hope here.*

" Ah, I dwelt, dwelt long in that abyss, driven by wild rage and a measureless despair. My death would then have seemed to me but my second death. Like Dante, during life, I passed through hell. But, to aid me also, a lady hastened down, before whose very look the evil spirits fear. Me, too, an angel from the pit redeemed. And I too had a Beatrice of my own.

" Oh, beautiful as she ! From this world of gloom thou didst not wing thy way, leaving me alone, to ascend to heaven—heavenly—to dwell there without pain. Oh, beautiful as she, thou wast more Christian far ! For there, where sorrow

---

* Chopin dedicated a piano concerto to Delphina Potocka ; and it was she who came and sang to him when he lay dying.

groweth, there, where tears are born, there, thou with thy brother didst remain upon this earth. Together walked we, wearing the self-same crown of thorns. Blood from my hands with blood empurpled thine. And the same empoisoned draught of one hellish spring, we did drink together, oh, Beatrice of mine.

" And yet, and yet my groaning and thy sighs, mingled with each other, they passed away to song. From two sorrows linked in bridal of the soul, one only voice was raised—and oh! that voice was joy. Ah! joyousness of faith, ah! mighty strength of hope, that into my heart returned by thy look! So do clouds of darkness, full of tears above, meet each other for a funeral in the skies. Light is torn forth from their weeping by a blast of thunder; and the mist becomes the golden house of God."

Dawn consists of a series of lyrics. Their subjects are love, self-sacrifice, and suffering, considered as a road of glory that leads to Poland's mystic triumph. But though the application is to Poland, Krasinski's nationalism, as I have already pointed out, touches so closely the mysticism of the human soul that *Dawn* does not speak only to one nation. Its message is universal.

Krasinski and his Beatrice are alone together in a boat on an Italian lake. Above them are the eternal snows of the Alps, the skies of Italy.

" There is one beauty and one God," cries the poet, in joy that was rarely his. With harp in hand and inspired eyes, Beatrice stands silvery, transfigured, as though rapt to heaven, in the light of the moon rising over the snows.

" Thou with me and we alone.
Oh, the angels cannot feel
What I feel now in this hour.
Sister mine, to me it seemeth
That our holy one* ariseth
At this moment from the coffin."

If only a dream, let him dream on. Let him and
her be of good heart, for, before the miracle shall
descend that will save them, they will not allow
their hearts to bleed for doubt, their brows to
grow heavy with fear. In the inspiration of their
common dreams, driven by the storm of pain in
the sorrows of this changing life, " within, beyond
them, we feel God."

" We are the children of a mother slain, we
who never have beheld how a mother's eyes shine
as an angel's on her child." They look to heaven
as an orphan looks. Moon, stars, and sun, nature's
beauty which is about them, as the boat cleaves
its way through the water, all make up one great
harp. Only the name of Poland is wanting to the
harmony of the universe. But, as God is in heaven,
even so will He restore her once again.

" To-day or to-morrow Thou wilt grant it to
us, Lord ! Oh, grant it for Thy justice sake ;
because Thou owest it, not to us, but to Thyself."

" When I spoke thus, thou wast kneeling,
Wailing with thy harp's stringed wailing ;
For thou leanedst thy snow-white forehead
On the strings the moon made shiver
All around in streams of gold.

* Poland.

And, thus kneeling, thou wast sighing.
Pray, oh, sister, with thy sighing.
God knows well that in this day
Sighing is thy country's name."

That country died a victim for the world's sin.
" Think you that who loves and dies can
perish ? To your eyes, to eyes of dust, but not
in sooth, nor to the universal life. Who died in the
hour of sacrifice has but passed into the lives of
others, and dwells in the hiding place of human
hearts ; and with each day, each little moment,
living, shall grow within that tomb, giving to all
and giving self." Invisible, she shall " burn with
fire the stones of hearts, soften with tears the
rocks of souls, and, by the sorrows and toils of the
grave, by the harmonious song of death, she shall,
though herself torn asunder, unite the nations in
one love."

The body has been slain. But " know you not
that in the world of the spirit love and death are
one ? Eternal is he who by his death gives birth
to life. But whoso by his life gives death he when
he dies shall rise no more."

Then the apostle of the ideal, of spiritual forces,
pours forth his wrath upon the wielders of brute
might and those who seek to corrupt the soul.

And now begins the series of his visions. He had
been parted, as he once said to a friend, by the
sword of Damocles from the land of his youth ;
and he asks of Beatrice :

" Knowest thou the love which eternally lures
the soul into the land of memory ? Does the cry
of the angel of thy country call thee by night, and

bid thee gaze into the living faces of those long
dead ? " He leads her in fancy to the snow-
covered steppe where the bones of his ancestors
rest, above which shine the moon and one star
—the Polar star of the north.

> " 'Neath the earth is mournful ringing.
> The burial place is trembling, living.
> From the graves blow prayers and wailing.
> Somewhere, swords are rattling hollow.
> Clash of armour stern I hear,
> As if our fathers, life remembering,
> Turning on their sides, were dreaming
> In death's sleep of Poland's sorrows."

The tombs give up their occupants. Kings,
knights, senators arise. The poet falls upon his
face before them, weeping. What did they do
with their lives that they left to their descendants
neither power nor inheritance, only instead of a
country a dismembered body ? A loud cry of
wrath goes up from the ghosts. The wraith of
Czarniecki, the great soldier of John Casimir's
days, answers that he grew, not from ease and
pleasure, but through pain. " To whom the Lord
gives torments He lays down His promises." It
is not for the poet to seek the fault in his fathers.
They lived in their age as guests of other ages.
Fate was driving them to a higher calling : " To
the Poland which *shall be*. And from our blood
and from our sins, before this age shall pass away
shall rise the one people of the peoples."

The steppe and the sky tremble and fade into
dreamland. The poet and Beatrice again float

upon the lake. The moon has sunk under a pall
of clouds. Surely that murmur they hear is no
sigh of the wind. A voice is weeping. The night
breeze carries to their ears a thousand wails. The
shores, the heights, become one prayer. The
spirits of the Polish dead are to appear to them
once more.

> "On the waters there before us,
>   Like light dreams, a fluttering throng,
>   On the rocks and crags they float.
>   As will-o'-the-wisps, as wavering flamelets,
>   Now they sink, and now they rise."

The poet cries to Beatrice to strike upon her
harp ; to tear from the strings with the sound of
thunder the song of the legions : *Poland hath not
perished*. The voice of the harp rushes over the
water, throbbing in Krasinski's verse with the
music and the word echoes of the Polish language,
that make the passage impossible for English
rendering. The vast army appears to the watchers'
eyes. There wave the insignia of Poland's warfare,
the horsetails, the white plumes, terrible in many
a Polish charge, shields, banners, and coats of
arms, with the cross towering above all. In the
midst, the face of the Mother of Christ :

> " As a star upon the darkness,
>   On high, on high suspended, rises,
>   Waning, glimmering, quivering, flaming.
>   Lo ! her veil of blue and crimson
>   Shines about her as a rainbow.
>   Set with pearls, and set with flowers,

Flashes out her crown of diamonds.
Welcome, welcome ! to the Queen,
Long a widow of her people,
To-day returning to her kingdom
Which, in Polish Czenstochowa,
Once our fathers gave to her.
And these fathers o'er the billows,
Lo, she leadeth." *

Let the harp cease. Its power sinks silenced
before that celestial rainbow. God's light has
touched the army of spirits. Dawn sparkles on
their helmets. The wings on their armour shine
as those of angels. In their glittering battle array
they sweep, with swords upraised in her defence,
after their queen. She has descended to crush the
serpent's head for the second time. The hour of
mercy has struck. " Now, oh, now, and for all ages,
God will wipe our tears away."

The heavenly hosts pass, and disappear into the
east, the dawn. They have gone, with their hope
and the light as of a more splendid day that lit
the lake and mountains. All is now dark, as before.
But in the poet's heart they have left faith and
joy. " All is mine," cries he to Beatrice ; " all is
fair. Mine the earth, the plains of heaven. I ring
forth the voice of life, for God's word is in my
heart. My Poland, Poland *shall be !* Praised be

* In gratitude for the repulse of the Swedes in 1655 at the walls
of Czenstochowa, which saved Poland, John Casimir proclaimed
the Blessed Virgin as Queen of Poland, and under that title she is
still addressed by the Polish nation. The ancient Byzantine
Madonna in the church of Czenstochowa has been for centuries
specially venerated by the Poles, and is described by Krasinski in
the above passage.

all and everything. Praised be through the ages unto ages God, the spirits, man, and thou, and praised the dead within their graves, and praised be all who are alive, and praised the universal world for ever, evermore! And to the skies will I repeat: 'Praise to Thee, Lord, I am happy.'"

The third vision follows: neither on the waters or mountains or clouds, but in some fathomless region, where no man can say. We have here a piece of pure Messianism. Krasinski sees his country, immortal, glorious, as the archangel of humanity. The purple garland of dolorous memories engirdles her brow; but her pain is over, and the spirit of God flashes as lightning from her countenance, and her fetters hang shattered. Beyond her is the countless multitude of the nations to which her sufferings shall give birth, crowned with the verdure, not of the things that are past, but of new hope and life, all doing homage to Poland as their queen. God's voice proclaims that she, who descended to the grave as a unit, rises in the day of victory re-baptized by the name of all humanity, with God's thought entrusted to her, by which she shall lead the world to its higher spirituality. As one god-like thought, the poet beholds the universe flame, the all-present, formless, endless glory of God, stars upon stars, suns upon suns. Through worlds of light, where one great hymn of praise thunders forth, lies the path of the nations to their Creator: and the poet looks upon his Poland leading the procession on this road, till she is lost to sight in the immensity of God.

" Whose eye
Can overtake her to those heights ?
Who shall bow his earthly forehead
On the feet of the Creator ?
Who shall soar with the archangel
Where humanity takes flesh ?
Now my heart faints in my bosom.
The image fades, my thought is failing.
Oh, so madly I entreated,
Oh, so long I prayed to God
For that one, that only moment :—
And I saw !

"In that hour,
Oh, remember that we were
On the highest height of souls—
There, whence flows the source of life.
At the source of life we drank.
With our very eyes we grasped
What is still without a name.
Sister mine, we, in that moment,
Lived in our eternity.

" Throw off sadness, throw off terror.
Well I know what toil remaineth
On the road ; what pain, what sorrow.
Trust thee to the poet's vision.
The dawn of victory now shines.

" In our native land, immortal,
On that soil so dearly loved,
On that soil, that soil of ours,
Shall arise a race renewed,"

to work the will of God in the government of the
universe, to bring back brotherly love, to trans-
form the earth.

> " Then that new world all rejoicing,
>   As a church shall flower to God.
>   The Polish land, the Polish Eden,
>   The desert of an agelong sadness,
>   Is desolate no more nor mourning.
>   Nor behind me nor before me
>   Is there darkness any more.
>   All is light and all is justice.
>   Clear is now our hallowed past,
>   Clear our purgatorial anguish,
>   And our sorrows and our bondage."

Poland cannot die, for she has risen above the
storms of this world to the land of the idea. They
who do not live by the idea shall perish without
hope. All that is visible to the eye alone must be
destroyed, " but the idea shall not pass away."
Therefore, she who is the representative and the
torchbearer of the idea is to him no longer merely " a
country, a place, a home," but " faith and truth."

So, at last, he has found that answer to which
he had journeyed through the fires of mental
travail and distress. God's ways are justified. The
sufferings of the nation that had wrung the hearts
of those who loved her are sanctified, and made
fruitful and glorious for herself and all mankind.

> " God Eternal of our fathers !
>   Thou, Who high and far away,
>   Ever clearer through the ages
>   Descendest to us, and, dawn-like, strewest

From the eternal gates Thy sparks
O'er time's waves until time flameth !
Now, again, Thy dawn is dawning
Which Thou in Thy love dost grant us.
In the graves the bones shall tremble
Sighing in a hymn to Thee.

" For our souls' and bodies' sufferings,
For our hundred years of torment,
We do give Thee thanks, oh, Lord.
We are poor and weak and feeble,
But, from this martyrdom of ours,
Has begun Thy reign on earth."

And the poet ends his poem in a pæan of
ecstasy and joy, which is doubtlessly inspired not
only by a national hope, but by the deliverance
of his own soul from the shadow of death in which
he had dwelt. The might of Satan's rule is no
more. The weak are oppressed no longer. Earth
is one song of harmony and rejoicing. The dark
days behind us were only a dreadful dream.

" Long the power of that dream.
We believed it. We believed
In eternal pain and toil.
They were but the sanctuary's entrance ;
But one step upon the stairway.
They were but the night of merit.

" Human heart, where now thy shame ?
Look into thyself, oh, gaze !
Where of old was rage and weeping,
Groans and cries and lamentation,
Lo, to-day of heaven's high mercy
Is the second house of God."

Forbidden by the censor, this poem yet found its way into Poland, and was watered with the tears of those who read.*

IV

In *Dawn* Krasinski had found his standpoint and never modified it. His subsequent teaching was rather in the nature of crystallizing his warnings to his people in special moments of national necessity; of reducing his general principles to practice. He had in his epilogue to *Dawn* said he would sing no more, for the only prayer worthy of the Creator knows no division between thought and deed. " Never, never again will I string my harp. Other are the roads that lie open before us. Perish, my songs ! Arise, my deeds ! " But in Krasinski's relations with his nation his poetry was his deed. He wrote not so much from a poet's inspiration as from a patriot's. He had no vision of literary fame. When the voice of Poland called, he wrote for her sake. At other times he remained silent.

The Psalms of the Future, which followed *Dawn*, are, therefore, in a manner episodical. But Krasinski is never merely topical or individual. He spoke seventy years ago. While these words are being written during the most terrible convulsion of modern times, the language and the tenets of the Polish poet rise instinctively to the mind, as almost strangely apposite to the needs and events of the hour.

* S. Tarnowski, *Zygmunt Krasinski*.

The first in order of date in the cycle of the *Psalms* is the *Psalm of Love*. The *Psalm of Faith* and the *Psalm of Hope* were written shortly afterwards as a sort of introduction to the third Psalm. We will therefore take them first. The occasion of all three Psalms, and most especially of the *Psalm of Love*, was Krasinski's foreboding of the danger that threatened his country from the democratic propaganda that was then proceeding.

As the title implies, the *Psalm of Faith* (1845) is Krasinski's confession of personal and national faith, and of his belief in the relations of God with the future of humanity.

The soul casts off the body and mind, worn out by a thousand trials. Men call that moment death ; but it is her second birth. She does not die. Taking to herself new and " unwearied wings," she soars into a higher region, leaving behind her the waning tracts of the past, with before her the endlessly stretching fields of measureless space, till she reaches " Him Who is all and enfoldeth all, the beginning and the end of Heaven and of earth."

" To Him I travel without pause. Thither must I first go through the pains of hell, through the toils of Purgatory, till I begin to put me on body and soul more radiant, and ascend to the other world. There, is eternal life and life unceasing." Hymning Paradise, as the desire of God, " love without bounds, that is life without end," he turns to the contemplation of Him Who is " Being, Thought, and Life, the Father, Son, and Holy Ghost. And we in His image must live immortally, must live together with Him, born of

His bosom to live in His eternity." As He created us, we must create and draw from ourselves that which He has given to us to create. " Inasmuch as we can, poor, in angelic lowliness, that which Thou gavest us of Thy mercy, we must give back to Thee, oh, God, and thus live eternally in Thee by eternal love."

This, then, leads up to Krasinski's national and political mysticism. " The history of humanity is the school of the soul." Christ will judge the nations on the day of resurrection ; for to each of these nations has been given some deep thought from the heart of the Creator, as their special predestined work for the human race. " And some are chosen before all others to combat for Thy beauty on the earth ; to carry the cross in a bloodstained track ; to give out the more love and greater brotherhood in exchange against the murderer's knife."

" Such a one, oh, God, is Thy Polish nation. Tho' the world gives her such pain that she could even doubt of hope, may she hold out in this unheard of suffering. For she is surely anointed in Thy spirit, for she is surely Thy high priest on this earth, if she will understand that Thou lovest without bounds those sons whom Thou dost crown with thorns ; for the thorn, steeped in blood, is the everlasting flower, and with it Thou shalt renew the youth of all humanity."

He concludes with a mystical analogy between the history and the calling of the human race, and the Divine pattern of Him Who came to save it.

" Christ ever dwelleth in thee, oh, humanity. His blood is thine. His body is thy body. With thee shall be what did befall to Him. He bore all thy vicissitudes within His flesh. To thee He manifested all thy hopes. Whence art thou born ? From a pure virgin womb, because from God's own thought in godly likeness. Whither dost thou go ? To thy Father's city. By what road must thou pass ? Through pain and labour. And when Christ on the summit of Mount Thabor was wrapped around with the eternal dawn, seest thou not what that sign to thee foretelleth ? Thou, too, oh, human race, shalt be transfigured. Thou shalt leave at the foot of the dark mountains all that deceives, and all that is of sorrow ; and thou shalt take spiritual knowledge with thee, and the eternal, unending love of hearts. And, in the strength of these two holy powers, as Christ shalt thou ascend to globes of light. All sin shall be erased from thy forehead. Light as feathers shall thy wings be. Thy hands shalt thou stretch forth on the white air, and in it shalt thou poise— as air thyself."

Having enunciated his dogma of faith, Krasinski proceeded to its natural sequence—the *Psalm of Hope*. Here, for once, there is scarcely a trace of the sadness, which overshadows the work of the poet whose heart was broken with sorrow for his nation.

" Long enough," thus opens the *Psalm of Hope*, " has the grief of the poets sounded the strings. Now is it time to strike on a second string, on the steel of deeds."

The poem is instinct with life, freshness and joy. The Revealer, the promised Paraclete, is nigh. With Him will begin the third and spiritualized

M

epoch. It is not the thrones or crowns who will be the first to perceive the advent of the Consoler, but she who, guiltless, is martyred. Then neither the merchant's cupidity, nor the executioner's hand, can prevail against Him Who is to change the universe.

"Oh, come more quickly, spring of the world! Oh, come more quickly, God the Spirit! Farewell, oh, earth, with thy pain and with thy mourning. The new Jerusalem is shining on the vale of this old earth. The road was long, and the toil heavy. A sea of tears and blood has flowed. But the angelic time draws near. Poland! thy grave was only as the cradle of the dawn.

"Tear aside the cloud of ages. Let us praise the Lord Who comes. Strew ye palms and strew ye psalms, flowers below and songs on high. Oh, cast songs and cast ye flowers! Lo, He comes, the Lord is coming. Now no more the Man of sorrows, choosing thorns and nails and wounds"; but "transfigured, from beyond the starred walls of the universe, as the blue all-horizon," He comes.

"Oh, drink ye with your souls that heavenly blue. Though you are tortured, you are tempted, oh, believe ye in my hope."

But neither here nor elsewhere in Krasinski's teaching will he allow that hope to be anything but conditional. It is to be proved in the fires of action. It is to be secured only at the price of individual and national self-discipline. "From your faith shall your will be, from your will shall your deed be." And on his trumpet note, "It is time to strike on the steel of deeds," the *Psalm of Hope* concludes.

We know how the Polish Rising, projected in the forties of the nineteenth century on democratic lines, was pushed by Austrian machinations into a different movement, and ended in the Galician massacres. Krasinski's piercingly clear political acumen was never obscured by the mystic tendency of his mind. He saw whither a class agitation would be likely to lead a nation groaning as was Poland under abnormal and intolerable conditions. Before the disaster befell, trembling for the moral danger that threatened his country, Krasinski sent forth a passionate cry to those of his fellow Poles, who were working a national rising as a social revolution, to stay before it was too late. That warning is his *Psalm of Love*. The *Psalm of Love* is a plea to the human race, no less than to one people, to shun the works of bloodshed and violence : the poet's attestation that one only element can save a nation, namely, love.

" Carry your arms against hell. Slay the black brood of demons. The guillotine and pillage are the weapons of the human race in its infancy ; rage, the liberty, not of man, but of the beast. Now is the time to take to oneself the toil of angels, the time to cast off every stain, and by that very act to conquer slavery. Destruction is not action. There is but one truth, divine, fruitful in deed ; transfiguration through love."

With his soul's whole strength, he pleads that the Poland he loved to call holy, who he believed was to prove to mankind that virtue and love are stronger than brute force, must never, by stooping to unworthiness and violence, lose her destined vocation.

" Who changeth sorrow into crime, who forgeth fetters into knives, not into swords, cursed be he."

" When geniuses have descended to this world, they have led their cause by a different road. No one of them was a dictator of the ages through murder and the torture chamber. Rather, they live in peril, in the end they die, but their victory lasts for ever. Only the weak soul chooses butchery. His name is Marius, his name is Robespierre."

Then he bids such of his countrymen who would sweep away the ancient nobility of Poland to look upon what the latter have done for their country. They have died for Poland in battle. They have perished for her in Siberia. And who, asks the poet, could we find who are faultless ? " Only one, He only Who was man and God ; and from the sinner another man soars upward through suffering, changed as the phœnix, and immortal." Search the world ; the Alps, the waters of the Mediterranean, the Spanish sierras, the snows of Russia, the battlefields of France, where the Polish nobles have sown " the seed of future Poland, the god-like grain, their own blood ; and you are the children of that pain." They lead that nation which, far from thrusting men down to the pit, is to uplift them as she mounts ever higher. But near her stands the tempter. Evil thoughts " grow where there are chains." Siberia and the knout are nothing to the poison sown by slavery. " But the corrupted spirit of a nation, that only is the pain of pains " ; conscience warped by a mass of suffering, reason confused by the wandering of perverted pride, crime represented as virtue, children taught to look on murder as a glorious deed, the sister bidding the brother take up the assassin's dagger, the native country turned into a hell.

"Oh, my holy one, abjure these delusions, the phantoms of an evil moment. Thou wilt not rid thee of thy ancient faith, that he only can cut through his chains who is anointed with the sign of virtue, that to be a Pole upon this earth is to live nobly and to God."

The Anonymous Poet reads hope from the very afflictions that thronged around his nation on every side.

"My Poland! Holy Poland! Thou standest on the threshold of thy victory. This is the last term of thy sorrows. Let it be only seen that thou art the eternal foe of evil. Then shall the chains of death be shattered, and thou wilt be assumed to heaven, because even in death thou wast with God."

In the final moment when death struggles with life, when dying lips sob out the last accents of doubt and lamentation :

"In the strength of thy martyrdom overcome that moment, conquer that pain ; and thou shalt rise again, thou shalt rise as the queen of the Slavonian fields."

Then the poet turns to the ideal of Messianistic longings ; the celestial vision of a spiritualized country.

"Let them who love thee gaze on thy face as on the spring. Be the mistress who straightens the crooked things of the world, the leader of universal love. Blot out all sin, dry all tears, rule over the world of souls, spurn the government of flesh. Unpolluted, carry the breath of the Lord."

But that spiritual conquest is not reached yet. The powers of darkness are still close at hand. "Fling away your murderous weapons," is the reiteration that tolls all through the concluding verses of the psalm. "Against hell carry your arms. Slay the black brood of demons." And, when the word of the Lord shall thunder forth, "then forward in the name of God" to the holy rising, from which "God will not turn away His face."

So ends the poem which Count Tarnowski places among the world's splendid failures of patriotic pleading,* written to save a nation, and written in vain.

The catastrophe, greater even than what Krasinski had foretold, came to pass in 1846. Krasinski beheld the country, whose purity and suffering he had promised would confer upon her the heralding of a new spiritual epoch, dragged down to shame. His anguish brought him to the point of death. From that time he was prematurely aged. Rent by the distress of his soul under which his bodily frame came near to sinking, in the agony of those days when Galicia was soaked in blood spilt by her own children, he could still, he did still, cling to the conviction of his heart. He could still tell the beloved friend to whom he poured out his thoughts that the idea would conquer.† He could still, apparently a dying man, tear from his pain words of consolation for his

---

* S. Tarnowski, *Zygmunt Krasinski.*
† *Letters of Zygmunt Krasinski.* Vol. I. To Constantine Gaszynski, March 1st, 1846.

people. And so he gave his nation her *Psalm of Grief*.

Slowacki, formerly Krasinski's friend, had, in a poem of extraordinary artistic beauty, made mockery, not untouched by a personal gibe at the Anonymous Poet's private tragedy, of the anti-revolutionary tendency of the *Psalm of Love*. The *Psalm of Grief* is Krasinski's justification against his brother-poet's attack. In grave and dignified accents, with the generosity of one who passed over the bitterness of an individual wound, Krasinski answers the poem that he himself praised as an ornament to the Polish language. Would, says he, that he had been the false prophet, and that his challenger had been the true one! On the lines of the *Psalm of Love*, he refutes the revolutionary tenets that he believed could only bring a nation to ruin. The spirit and the flesh ever war, the idea against the brute beast, the angel against the tiger. In the combat and convulsion of the world, who shall redeem us? Who shall bring harmony into a disordered chaos? He Who knows neither the burden of the body nor the sickness of the soul: the Holy Ghost. Beneath His rule blood will be shed no more. "In the morning He waketh to hope the people who slumber." He shall make the very shadows " as silver, till dawn becomes midday."

Brotherly love will save those who are trembling on the very brink of the abyss. Parted from each other, they are damned. United, they are redeemed. The radiance of the Holy Ghost conquers the curse of centuries. The soul, ruled by Him, "shall feel the love of toil and the courage of suffering."

She shall " lift men from the mire and hide their shame. Unabased in the midst of vileness, loving ever in the midst of trials, her heart will become as steel, and her eyes shall weep for every human grief." Thus through love and pain shall the soul work her way to God. Even with the horror of what had recently befallen fresh upon him; when to keep hope alive, where every exterior event incited to despair, meant a life and death struggle, the Anonymous Poet spoke a message of virility and life. He bade his people be the nation to rise above moral stain, whose weapon shall not be the assassin's but Christ's, and who will therefore conquer in the power of Christ ; whose triumph shall be commensurate with her anguish and her love. " Thus she riseth from the dead ": are the last words of the *Psalm of Grief*.

With the *Psalm of Good Will*—1848—Krasinski's *Psalms of the Future* close. This, the noblest of Krasinski's poems, is the seal of his life's work, the culmination of the great prophetical poetry of Poland. His own pain had taught Krasinski his message to his nation. The *Psalm of Good Will* breathes the sadness and majesty of a farewell to his people, from one who had won to his haven after suffering and struggle. In its long, sweeping cadences the hymn reveals that the poet had looked into the mysteries of grief only to rise victorious above them ; that he had found in death no sting but resurrection. His prayer is not for his nation's glory, not for her material triumph, but for that which will bring her both : for good will.

" Now that Thy judgment has thundered in

heaven on the two thousand years that have past, amidst that judgment, grant us, oh, Lord, that by our holy deeds we may rise from death."

This is the petition of which the poet cannot weary, to which the stanzas of the Psalm modulate as into some grand closing chord.

"Thou hast given us all that Thou couldst give, oh, Lord," sings the son of the unhappiest of nations. With the eyes of mystical devotion, he reads in her past a history of love. "Thou hast given us all that Thou couldst give, oh, Lord"; for, when thrust down from the land of the living by dismemberment, "Thou didst keep us who were dead living in the field of war. We were not, and we were. . . . Thou hast given us all that Thou couldst give, oh, Lord; a pure life, therefore worthy of the cross, and the cross that brings us to Thy stars. Earth Thou didst take from us, and send down heaven, and Thy heart shelters us on every side. But our free will Thou hadst to leave to us. Without ourselves, even Thou canst not save us; for so hast Thou ennobled man and every nation that Thy thought, suspended in heaven, awaits the choice of man or nation for their several roads." "Thou hast given us all that Thou couldst give, oh, Lord"; the example of Jerusalem, "in whom Thy love for so long dwelt," and who is throneless and widowed because she desired revenge, and does not understand the might of Christ's cross. "Thou hast given us all that Thou couldst give, oh, Lord"; for we have seen how the works of death bring destruction, not on those against whom they are directed, but on those who handle them.

Here ends the tranquil and devout hymn of praise. Behind Krasinski's promises, there is always the reality of an exacting warfare. If Poland is to be a chosen nation, the harder must be her struggle to justify her calling. The Psalm becomes a supplication for victory in the battle.

"We are above the abyss, on the narrow straits. Our wings are sprouting to the resurrection, our lips are parted for the cry of joy. From the blue skies, as though from Thy bosom, golden shafts of dawn, as though Thy sheltering arms, are spreading from the heavens to us on earth below, to take from our foreheads the load of agelong sorrow. All is ready, and the east is all aflame, and angels watching."

But from the other side, heaving to our feet, rises the darkness : " the pit, eternal death, where Thou art not," where are all things evil. If we turn one backward glance towards it, one step to meet it, then " the light of dawn will pale upon our brows, Thy Son shall shed no tear for us, and the Holy Spirit shall not console us."

" Have mercy, Lord, defend us, be with us ! " We stand alone to face the final moment. None may help us. Our destiny is in our own hands.

Then the name, with which " upon their lips millions of Polish souls have gone to death," rises in the poet's heart : the name of Mary. He sees her, not with the rapture of his earlier vision in *Dawn*, leading in triumph a host of warriors, but as a suppliant, kneeling at the throne of her Son, pleading for a suffering nation. He sees her above the stars that turn to her in prayer, above suns and the Milky Way, and behind her, weeping, are the souls of the Polish dead. Below is the pit, echoing with the mocking laughter of hell. Its winds roar in our ears, the foam of its waves blinds our eyes by which it would drag us down to death. " Oh, vain one, it seeth not what is being wrought on high. Oh, vain one, it seeth not that its rage is nought when such a heart for us is wrung." And the poet then pours out his last prayer for his people :

" Oh, Lord, Lord, then not for hope—as a flower is it strewn : then not for the destruction of our foes—their destruction dawns on to-morrow's clouds : not for the weapons of rule—from the tempests they will fall to us : not for any help— Thou hast opened already the field of events before us : but amidst the terrible convulsion of these events, we beseech Thee only for a pure will within ourselves, oh, Father, Son, and Holy Ghost.

" Oh, Thou most dear, hidden but visible beyond the veils of the transparent worlds, Thou present everywhere, immortal, holy ! Thou Who commandedst the being of man that, poor in strength, and little in his birth, he should to an angel grow by might of sacrifice ; and to our Polish nation didst ordain that she should lead the nations into love and peace ! We beseech Thee, Father, Son, and Holy Ghost, we, suspended between Thy kingdom and the pit, we beseech Thee with our foreheads sunk to earth, our temples bathed in the breathing of Thy spring, surrounded with the wheels of shattered times and perishing governments, Father, Son, and Holy Ghost ! we beseech Thee create in us a pure heart, make new our thoughts within us, root out from our souls the tares of sacrilegious falsehood, and give us the gift, eternal among Thy gifts—give us good will ! "

One only word more remained to Krasinski to speak to his people, and then his work was done. In the thick of the terrible events of 1846, when, weighed down by physical weakness and mental agony, he could scarcely set pen to paper, he had struggled to send his nation the message she needed.

" Oh, pray for me to God," he wrote to Delfina Potocka, as his spirit wrestled against a mind and body too wearied to obey its bidding. " I feel nothing egotistic in that desire. For Poland "—whom even in a private letter he calls by a feigned name—" is bent beneath all the winds. She implores, she implores for counsel."* Dissatisfied with what he wrote, Krasinski did not publish the poem in question till 1851, when it came out under the title *Resurrecturis*. It stands forth as his supreme victory over pessimism and despair. What, he asks, is this world but a " cemetery of tears, of blood and mire ? This world is an eternal Golgotha to each. The spirit writhes in vain against its pain. There is no halting place in the tempest of this life. Fate mocks us every moment. Death is close ; and only far away, somewhere on a later wave of ages, resurrection.

" Then must we grow numb, be petrified, be without heart, become as murderers among the murderers, among the criminals be criminal ourselves ? Lie, hate, and slay, and mock. We will

* *Works of Zygmunt Krasinski*. Jubilee Edition, Cracow, 1912. Vol. VI. p. 369.

give back to the world what it gives us. Let us
eat and drink, caress the body and abase the mind.
So shall we be counted among the stupid and the
happy.

"Oh, let it not be so! My soul, draw back, oh,
stay! Not such a weapon for those who would
shorten evil. Only one power in the world, the
quiet strength of sacrifice, conquers an oppressive
fate.

"Oh, know thyself for what thou art. Crave
not for the mastery which is His in heaven, nor
choose to be as the brute beast fattening on the
fields of pasture. On this side the grave, before
the resurrection dawns, be thou an unbroken
masterpiece of will, be patience, mistress of misfortune, that slowly buildeth up an edifice from
nought. Be that defeat, of distant aim, but which
at last shall conquer for all ages. Be peace amidst
the raving of the storm, and harmony in discord.
Be thou eternal beauty in the eternal war of life.
Be as a sister's tears to those who sorrow, the
voice of manhood to those whose courage faints,
a home to the exile, hope to those who have lost
their hope. In the struggle with this hell of earth,
be ever, everywhere, the strength that against
death prevails with the stronger strength of love;
be thou the hell of love.*

"In word and in example give thyself freely
to thy brothers. Multiply thy one self by living
deeds, and from thy one self a thousand shall
come forth. Be thou even in chains by toil

---

* The critics took exception to the expression "hell of love."
Krasinski defended it, saying he had taken it from the writings of
St. Teresa. *Letters of Z. Krasinski to Stanislas Koźmian.* Lwów,
1912 (Polish).

unwearied. Let every pain, though it shall pain, not pain thee. Be sanctity in bondage.

"What the world called dream and mirage, make living, make of them a faith, a law, a certainty, a truth, till the world, thy murderer, shall kneel and own that God and country are as the conscience of the nations. Thy thought shall be the stream of light, God's judgment flashing on the heights, above the throng of godless here below. Nor men nor cannon shall keep it back, nor falsehood, nor deception, genius, praise, nor kings, nor peoples."

Thus the Anonymous Poet, who began his career with an *Undivine Comedy*, ended it with a *Resurrecturis*.* He was surrounded all his days by the tragedy of his nation, tormented within and without by the intolerable bitterness of a life, which to him, and to every Pole of his generation, brought nothing but the spectacle of all that was sacred and beloved trampled underfoot and unavenged. Every incitement to despair, revenge, negation of God and hatred of man, might well have been his. Yet he pointed without faltering to one great moral : to the triumph of hope, love, and pain over evil, to salvation through purity of aims and means. " In spite of all visible events," he wrote to his friend Gaszynski at a time when no ray of light pierced the cloud of tribulation that hung over Poland, and over his own life, " believe

---

* In a short sketch of this nature, I have been obliged to confine myself entirely to Krasinski's masterpieces, which are at the same time those that chiefly show the development of his idea. It is enough to say here, that those writings of his that I have had to pass over carry out the same thoughts, and breathe the same devoted patriotism.

me a better dawn is near, a second spring in our lives, another youth. Poland will give us back, will give us back what we have lost for her, joy, enthusiasm, the heart's health."* In each defeat he bade his nation see but the promise of her future victory. He believed against the cruellest evidence of circumstance. *Speravit contra spem.*

* *Letters of Zygmunt Krasinski.* Vol. I,   To Constantine Gaszynski, June 1, 1843.

CHAPTER V

THE MYSTIC PILGRIMAGE IN SIBERIA

AMONG the greatest of Poland's poets stands Julius Slowacki. Inferior to his contemporaries, Mickiewicz and Krasinski, in depth of thought or moral beauty, he is a master of style and language. He began his poetical life as a follower and warm admirer of Byron. He ended it—death took the brilliant, egotistic poet in the flower of his years—as a mystic.

" Place on his grave for all inscription : To the author of *Anhelli ;* and that will be enough to secure his fame in future generations." So wrote Krasinski after Slowacki's death.* And *Anhelli,* that strange mystical and poetic journey through Siberia, stamped with the eternal despair of the prison-house of the Pole, ranks with the most striking and most tragic productions of the great prophetic-national Polish literature.

"When I read it," said Krasinski—and it should be remembered that one of Krasinski's lifelong tortures was his terror of Siberia added to his conviction that he would be banished there—" I yearned, God help me ! for Siberia. For many nights, Siberia appeared to me in my dreams as a melancholy Eden."† " The stamp of his

---

* A. Malecki, *Julius Slowacki.* Lwów, 1901 (Polish).

† *Letters of Zygmunt Krasinski.* Vol. III. Lwów, 1887. To Roman Zaluski, May 13th, 1840 (Polish).

[Slowacki's] poetry," he goes on to say, " is that marvellous mingling of horror and of charm."

The impression made by *Anhelli* on the reader's mind is that of a desolation as unending as those dreary snow-bound wastes that Slowacki unrolls to our gaze ; a despair which the pale light of the vague mysticism that gleams through the work seems but to enhance. The white deserts, their sameness only broken by the figures of the doomed Polish exiles ; the fires of the Northern lights ; the strange brilliance of the Siberian winter stars, are a fit setting for Anhelli, the youth who passes through the prisons and the mines, as the type of his people's sufferings, till his heart breaks with his anguish.

It is not our intention to describe Slowacki's *Anhelli*, but to let this exquisite prose-poem speak for itself in extracts which can, unfortunately, convey but a meagre impression of the beauty of the Polish original. But we would first note one or two of its characteristics. Inspired in part by Slowacki's wanderings in the Holy Land, it is written in a species of Biblical prose. It is in no wise intended as a closely exact presentment of Siberia. More than one of the episodes introduced into it belong, not to Siberia, but to Poland. Various of the Poles whom Anhelli meets in Siberia never in reality went there. But Slowacki chose to place the poem consecrated to the sorrows of his nation, and into which he poured his own sadness and weariness of life, in Siberia, that land watered by the tears of thousands of Poles, which, at the time that the poet was writing, stood before

N

Polish minds as the large factor with which they were compelled to reckon.*

Although, from time to time, *Anhelli* touches upon the Messianistic theory of Poland's salvation and exaltation, yet its general tone is that of a profound melancholy that borders on despair, of something, indeed, not far removed from pessimism that, as we have seen, is unusual in the Polish poetry of Slowacki's generation. We have called *Anhelli* a mystical poem ; but its mysticism is of a peculiarly indeterminate and unsatisfying description. In fact, with a few exceptions here and there, the supernatural element in *Anhelli* strikes the reader as being more of a fairy-like than, strictly speaking, a spiritual nature. This feature weakens the work as a great national expression ; but from the artistic standpoint it creates that weird and unearthly atmosphere that for long haunts our vision, as though we had wandered to some far distant and unutterably mournful dream-land.

"The exiles came into the land of Siberia," (so *Anhelli* begins). "And, clearing a wide place, they built them a wooden house, that they might dwell together in harmony and brotherly love. For some time there was great order among them and great sadness, because they could not forget that they were exiles, and would see their country no more, unless it pleased God."

Here Slowacki has the Polish Emigration in mind.† He describes how dissensions break out in their midst. Then :

"They saw a great flock of black birds flying

* A. Malecki, *op. cit.*   † A. Malecki, *op cit.*

from the north. And beyond the birds there appeared, as it were, a caravan, and a tribe of people, and sledges drawn by dogs, and a herd of reindeer with branching horns, and men on skates carrying spears. And at their head went the king of the tribe, who was also their priest, clad in furs and in corals.

" Then that king, as he drew nigh to the crowd of exiles, said to them in the language of their own country : ' Welcome ! Lo, I knew your fathers, unhappy like you ; and I beheld how they lived in the fear of God and died, saying, Oh, my country ! my country ! ' "

This king, the Shaman, the Siberian wizard-priest, stays with the exiles to comfort them. He is the Virgil of the poem, who leads Anhelli through the journey where he is confronted, not so much with individuals, as in the *Divina Commedia*, but with the symbolizations of the national sufferings.*

" Then the Shaman, gazing into the hearts of that band of exiles, said within himself : ' Verily, I have not found here what I sought. Their hearts are weak, and they will be vanquished by sadness. They would have been worthy men in the midst of happiness, but misery will change them into evil and dangerous men. Oh, God, what hast Thou done ? Dost Thou not grant to every flower to bloom where it finds its own life and its own soil ? Why, then, must these men perish ? I will, therefore, take one from among them, and I will love him as a son, and when I die I will lay upon him my burden, and a greater burden than others can

* A. Malecki, *op. cit.*

bear, that in him there shall be redemption. And I will show him all the sorrows of this earth, and then I will leave him alone in a great darkness, with the load of thought and of yearning in his heart.'

" When he had said this, he called to him a youth of the name of Anhelli and, laying his hands upon him, he poured into him heartfelt love and pity for men. And, turning to the crowd of exiles, he said : ' I will depart with this youth to show him many sorrowful things, and you shall remain alone to learn how to bear hunger, misery and sadness. But keep hope. For hope shall go forth from you to the future generations and will give them life : but, if it dieth within you, then the future generations will be as dead men. Keep watch upon yourselves, for you are as men standing upon a height, and they who are to come will behold you. But I say unto you, be at rest, not about the morrow, but about the day which will be the morrow of your death. For the morrow of life is more bitter than the morrow of death.' "

" You are as men standing on the height," said Slowacki. Here we have the Messianistic theory of the Pole's vocation. The poet's insistence on hope is also characteristic of the mystic national literature and of the whole temper of his nation. Hope preserved the life of Poland.

The hour has struck for Anhelli to set forth on his pilgrimage through the house of bondage of his people. The Shaman summons him from slumber, bidding him " ' Sleep not, but come with me, for there are things of import in the desert.'

" Then Anhelli, clothing himself with a white

robe, followed the old man, and they walked in the light of the stars. . . .

" And the Shaman passed with Anhelli through the desert ways of Siberia where were the prisons. And they saw faces of prisoners, pallid and sorrowful, looking through the gratings to the sky. And near one of the prisons they met men carrying biers, and the Shaman stayed them, bidding them open the coffins. When, then, they had taken the lids off the coffins, Anhelli shuddered, beholding that the dead were still in their fetters, and he said : ' Shaman, I fear lest these martyred men shall not rise from the dead. Awaken one of them, for thou hast the power of working miracles. Wake that old man with the hoary beard and white hair, for it seems to me that I knew him when he was alive.' And the Shaman, with a stern look, said : ' Wherefore ? I will raise him from the dead, and thou wilt slay him again. Verily, twice will I raise him up, and twice he will die at thy hands. But let it be as thou wilt, that thou mayest know that death shelters us from sorrows which were waiting for us on the road, but which found us dead.'

" Speaking thus, the Shaman looked upon the old man in his coffin, and said : ' Arise ! ' And the body in chains rose and sat up, gazing at the people like a man that sleeps."

But as Anhelli repeats to this man—Niemojowski, a well-known figure in the Polish history of Slowacki's time, and one whom the poet knew personally—some of the tales that were told against him, " he who had risen from the dead died again, wailing."

" Then the Shaman said : ' Anhelli, thou hast slain him by repeating men's slanders and calumnies, of which he knew not before his death. But I will raise him up a second time, and do thou beware lest thou bring him a second time to his death.'

" He awoke the dead man, and he rose in his coffin, with tears streaming from his open eyelids."

Mindful of the wizard's warning, Anhelli begs the dead man's forgiveness, and speaks words of praise both of him and of his equally famous brother. " ' Oh, unhappy ye,' " he ends. " ' Lo, one seeketh rest in a Siberian graveyard, and the other lies under the roses and cypresses on the Seine—separated and dead.'

" When he had heard these words, the man who had risen from the dead cried out : ' Oh, my brother !' and he fell back in the coffin, and died. And the Shaman said to Anhelli : ' Why didst thou tell him of his brother's death ? One moment, and he would have known it from God, and he would have met his beloved brother in the heavenly land. Let them close the coffins and carry them to the cemetery. And ask me no more to raise from the dead those who are asleep and at rest.'

" And so the Shaman with Anhelli made their journey through the sorrowful land, and through the desert ways and beneath the murmuring forests of Siberia, meeting the suffering people and comforting them.

" And one evening they passed near still-standing water, where grew many weeping willows and a few pines."

And as the Shaman watched the little fish
" leaping to the afterglow," he conjures Anhelli
to bear in mind that melancholy " 'is a mortal
disease.'

" ' For there are two melancholies. One is
from strength, the other from weakness. The first
is as wings to men of high mind, the second a
stone to drowning men. I tell thee this because
thou art yielding to sadness, and thou wilt lose
hope.'

" While he still spoke, they came upon a throng
of Siberians who were catching fish in the lake.
And when the fishers had seen the Shaman, they
ran to him, saying : ' Oh, our king ! Thou hast
forsaken us for strangers, and we are sad because
we see thee among us no more. Stay with us this
night, and we will make thee a banquet.'

" But after the supper, when the moon rose
and threw her light over the smooth water,"
the Shaman, to revive the faith of these children
of the desert, works a miracle for them. He casts
Anhelli into a trance :

" Calling a little child from the crowd, he placed
him on the breast of Anhelli, who had laid him
down as though to sleep, and he said to the child :
' Lay thy hands on the forehead of this youth,
and call him three times by the name of Anhelli.'
And it befell that at the call of the child the soul
went forth from Anhelli, and it was of a fair form
and many hued colours, and had white wings on
its shoulders. And beholding itself freed the
spirit went on the water, and it fled across the
column of the moon's light towards the south.

" But when it was afar off and in the middle

of the lake, the Shaman bade the child call upon the soul to return. And the bright spirit looked back at the cry of the child, and it returned slowly over the golden wave, dragging after it the ends of its wings which were drooping for sorrow. And when the Shaman bade it descend into the body of the man, it wailed like a shattered harp and trembled, but it obeyed. And Anhelli, awaking, sat up and asked what had been wrought with him. The fishermen answered : ' Lord, we have seen thy soul. The Chinese kings are not clothed in such splendour as the soul that belongs to thy body. And we have seen nothing brighter on the earth save the sun, and nought glittering more brightly save the stars. The swans flying over our land in May have not such wings. Yea, and we even smelt scent like the scent of a thousand flowers.'

" ' What, then,' (asks Anhelli of the Shaman), ' did my soul when she was free ? ' The Shaman answered him : ' She went over that golden road that is cast on the water from the moon, and she fled to yonder side like one that is in haste.' And at these words Anhelli drooped his head, and, musing, he began to weep, and he said : ' She was fain to return to my country.' "

Having comforted Anhelli, the Shaman leads him on, he himself working fresh miracles, till, says he :

" ' Lo, we will show miracles no more nor the power of God that is in us : but we will weep, for we have come to the people who do not see the sun. We may not teach them wisdom, for sorrow has taught them more. Nor will we give them hope, for they will not believe us. In the decree that condemned them was inscribed : For ever ! Here are the mines of Siberia.'

" ' Step carefully here, for the earth is paved with sleeping men. Dost thou hear ? They breathe heavily, and many moan and talk in their sleep. One speaks of his mother, another of his sisters and brothers, and a third of his home and of her whom he loved in his heart, and of the meadows where the corn bowed to him as to its lord. And they are happy now in their sleep—but they will wake. In other mines criminals wail ; but this is only the grave of the sons of the nation, and is filled with silence. The chain that rattles here has a sorrowful sound, and in the vault there are many echoes, and one echo which says : I mourn for you.'

" While the Shaman was speaking thus pitifully, there came wardens and soldiers with lanterns to awaken the sleepers to labour. Then all rose up from the ground, and woke, and they went like sheep with bent heads, except one who rose not, for he had died in his sleep "—
having swallowed poisonous lead that he had picked up from the floor of the mine in the hope of ending his misery.

The pilgrims wend their way through the depths of the mines :
" Till they saw many men, pallid and tortured, whose names are known in our country. And they came to a subterranean lake, and trod the banks of its dark water which stirred not, and here and there was yellow from the light of the lanterns. And the Shaman said : ' Is this the

Sea of Galilee ? * And are these the fishers of woe ? '

" Then, one of those who sat sadly by the banks of the black water said : ' To-day they allow us to rest, because it is the Tsar's name-day. So we sit here over the dark water to dream and think and rest ; for our hearts are more weary than our bodies. And, not long since, we lost our prophet,† whose favourite place was this rock, and to whom these waters were dear. And seven years ago on a certain night the spirit of prophecy took possession of him, and he felt the great convulsion that there was in our country,‡ and he told us the whole night what he saw, laughing and weeping. And only at dawn did he wax sad, and he cried : Lo, they have risen from the dead, but they cannot roll away the stone from the sepulchre : and having said this, he fell dead.'

" And the Shaman, turning him to Anhelli, said : ' Why art thou thus lost in thought above this black water, which is of human tears ? '

" When he had spoken, there resounded a great echo from an explosion in the mine, and it was prolonged above their heads, beating like a subterranean bell. And the Shaman said : ' Behold the angel of the Lord for those who see the

* Slowacki wrote *Anhelli* under the influence of his journey in Palestine, dedicating the poem to the Pole who had been his fellow-traveller there. The Sea of Galilee was one of the spots that he had visited, and certain of his descriptive passages, such as the lake where Anhelli's soul is shown to the fishermen, are said to be the poet's impressions of the scenery of the Holy Land.

† Slowacki said that this prophet was an imaginary figure, but that at the same time he had Thomas Zan in his mind. When the poet wrote *Anhelli*, Zan was still in exile, but he returned in later years to end his days in his own country.

‡ The Rising of 1830, which took place eight years before *Anhelli* was published.

sun no more. Oh, God, oh, God, we pray Thee that our sufferings may be our redemption. And we will not entreat Thee to restore the sun to our eyes and the air to our lungs, for we know that Thy judgment has fallen upon us—but the newborn generation is guiltless. Have mercy, oh, God ! And forgive us that we carry our cross with sadness and that we rejoice not as martyrs ; because Thou hast not said if our suffering will be reckoned to us as our expiation. But speak the word, and we shall rejoice. For what is life that we should mourn for it ? Is it the good angel that leaves us in the hour of death ? Happy are they who may sacrifice themselves for the nation ! ' "

The Shaman and Anhelli pass on where all is sorrow. Here, they see an old man knouted to death, there, a Russian prince toiling as a felon, with his devoted wife ministering to him. At last, like a second Virgil with his Dante, the guide carries Anhelli up from the pit ; and Anhelli opens his eyes once more on the Siberian stars and snow, asking himself if what he had beheld was but a dreadful dream.

The scope of the poem now somewhat changes. The national sufferings recede further into the background, and the grief of Anhelli himself fills the poem ; a grief which, however, never ceases to be that of the Pole, eternally mourning for his nation. It is curious to notice that, as the poet departs from those great tragedies with which the heart of the Pole was filled when Slowacki wrote, and lingers instead on a more individual and restricted note, the artistic beauty of the work seems to increase rather than to be impaired.

In the forlorn figure of the youth, desolate and alone in the Siberian night, and painted with an almost terrible power, there is much of Slowacki himself. The tale of his own sad and lonely soul is told here.

As he gazes at the angel Eloe, who sits watching the graves of those who have died in Siberia, Anhelli falls like a dead man. When recalled to life by the Shaman, bidding him arise, for the time of his rest has not yet come, Anhelli confesses that the face of the angel reminds him of one whom he had loved in his own country.

" ' Therefore am I flooded with my tears when I think of her and of my youth. To-day that is all a dream. Yet the sapphire sky and the pale stars look down on me : are those stars in truth the same as those that saw me young and happy ? Why does not a gust of wind arise to tear me from the earth, and to carry me into the land of peace ? Why do I live ? There is not one hair on my head of those that there were of old, even the bones within me are renewed—and yet I still ever remember. And there is not one bird in the sky who cannot sleep, if but one night of its life, in a quiet nest. But God has forgotten me. I would fain die.' "

Thus he complains, wandering among the graves of those who died far from their country, and whose names are already forgotten. In the poet's first conception, Eloe was to represent fame ; not mere renown, but rather the spiritualized memory of the dead. But towards the end of *Anhelli*, Slowacki's idea modified her into a more human shape.*

* A. Malecki, *op. cit.*

The Shaman and Anhelli then leave the graveyard.

" And, when they came to the house of the exiles, they heard a great tumult and laughter and clamour, and the rattling of cups and foul songs : and the Shaman stood at the windows and listened, ere he entered that pit of misery. And, when he appeared amidst the band, they were silent, because they knew that man who was mighty in God, and they dared not defy him. And lifting his flashing eyes, the Shaman spoke, on fire for grief : ' What have ye done without me ? I have seen your Golgotha. Woe unto you ! The stormy winds scatter the seeds of the oak and strew them over the earth ; but cursed shall be the wind that carries your speech and your counsel to your country. You shall die. The great day* is drawing nigh, and none of you shall live to behold the eve of that day. The Siberian day and the sun of destruction draw nigh. Why have you not hearkened to my counsels, and lived peacefully in harmony and brotherly love, as befits those who have no country ? ' "

Where, in *Anhelli*, Slowacki describes, as he does more than once, the evils reigning among the exiles, it is his note of warning, for all its somewhat fantastic setting, against those moral dangers threatening a nation suffering and living in abnormal ways.†

In answer to his reproaches, the exiles set upon the Shaman and slay him. As he lies dying, he calls Anhelli and gives him his last charge.

" ' Take my reindeer and go to the north. Thou

---

* The day of Poland's resurrection.   † *Op. cit.*

wilt find a dwelling and peace in the snow. And thou shalt live on the milk of the reindeer. Be not sorrowful unto death for the destruction of thy country : but weep at the thought that thou shalt see her no more. All is a sorrowful dream.'"

He further tells Anhelli to take with him Ellenai, a woman once a sinner, who had ministered to the wizard's last moments, and to live with her as with a sister.

" As he spoke thus, Anhelli heard a trampling on the snow, and said : ' Some one approaches ; or is it death that walks heavily ? ' But it was a reindeer that stood above his dying master, and whose wondering eyes filled with great tears ; and the Shaman turned away from him, weeping."

He dies : and Anhelli leads Ellenai away :
" Both turned to the north, and behind them went the Shaman's reindeer, knowing that they were following new masters. But Anhelli was silent, for his heart was full of tears and of grief. So they went, Anhelli with the woman and with the Shaman's reindeer to the far northern desert ; and, finding an empty hut hewn out in the ice, they dwelt in it." And the heart of the woman " from continual prayer was full of tears, sadness, and heavenly hopes."

" Then the Siberian day came on, and the sun did not set, but ran through the sky like a horse at the race with a fiery mane and a white brow. The terrible light never ceased, and the noise of the ice was like unto the voice of God speaking on the heights to the sorrowful and forsaken people.

" And her long sadness and yearning led the exiled woman to her death, and she laid her down on a bed of leaves among her reindeer to die. And it was at the setting of the sun, because for some time past nights had begun in the land of Siberia, and the sun remained ever longer beneath the horizon. Turning her sapphire eyes filled with tears on Anhelli, Ellenai said : ' I loved thee, my brother, and I leave thee. I loved thee, but the grave ends all. Forget me not, for who will remember me after death save one reindeer which I milked ? '

" Then the dying woman began to recite litanies to the Mother of God and, even as she uttered the words *Rose of gold*, she died. And a fresh rose fell on the white bosom of the dead woman and lay there, and the strong fragrance of the rose filled the hut. But Anhelli sat at the side of the couch and wept. And lo, at midnight came a great rustling, and Anhelli thought that the reindeer made this rustling, drawing out moss to eat from under the bed of death ; but a cloud, as of the spirits of darkness, poised over the hut with loud laughter, and dark faces appeared through the clefts of the ice roof and cried : ' She is ours.' But that wondrous rose put on the wings of a dove and flew on high, and looked upon them with the eyes of a pure angel. So those dark spirits and the cloud of them arose from the roof, crying sad curses into the dark sky ; and again there was silence as befits the place where a dead body rests.

" And three hours after midnight Anhelli heard a knocking at the door, which was of ice, and, putting aside the block of ice, he went out under the moon. And he saw the angel who had recalled to him his love for a woman and his first love on the earth. And Eloe said to him : ' Give me thy dead sister : I will take her and bury her pitifully. She is mine.' And Eloe, kneeling over the sleeping figure, laid under her the ends of her swan wings, and, soaring to the moon, departed. Anhelli, therefore, returned to the empty hut, and mourned because she was there no more.

" Then about the time when the earth begins to turn from the sun and sleeps in darkness, Jehovah called two of the eternal Cherubim before His throne, and said : ' Go ye to the plains of Siberia.' And they went down into the misty land, hiding their brightness within them. And they came to the place where the shed of the exiles had been, but they found no trace of it, for the storms had brought it to the ground. And of those thousand men there remained but ten, pale and terrible to behold."

Starving in the snow, they had eaten human flesh, the bodies of their comrades. The leader of the survivors, with the blood of his countrymen on his lips, cries : " 'Has God remembered us ? Has He granted us to die in our land and on the earth where we were born ? '

" ' Return,' [reply the angels], ' and pray to God, for we will show you the sign of His wrath which was once the sign of pardon.' And, stretching out their hands, the angels pointed to a mighty rainbow which ran across half of the clouded skies. And a terrible fear took possession of the man-eaters at the sight of this beautiful and flashing thing. And, marvelling, they pronounced the name of Christ, and fell dead.

"That same day, before the setting of the sun, Anhelli sat on a block of ice in a desert place, and he saw two youths drawing nigh. Because of the light wind that came forth from them, he felt that they were from God, and he awaited what they would announce to him, expecting that it was death. And when they had greeted him like unto mortal men, he said : ' I know you. You are angels. Do you come hither to console me ? Or to quarrel with my sadness which I have learned in the solitude of silence ? '

"And the youths said to him : ' Behold, we have come to announce to thee that the sun of to-day will rise again, but to-morrow's shall show itself no more over the earth. We have come to announce to thee the winter darkness and a greater horror than any men have ever known, solitude in darkness. We have come to announce to thee that thy brothers are dead, having eaten of human corpses and being maddened with human blood : and thou art the last. And we are the same who ages ago came to the hut of the wheelwright,* and sat at his table in the shade of the sweet smelling lime-trees. Your nation was then as a man who waketh and saith to himself : Lo, a fair thing awaits me at midday, and in the evening I shall rejoice. We announced hope unto you, and now we have come to announce the end and sorrow, and God hath not bidden us reveal the future.'

"And Anhelli, answering, said to them : ' Are

* Piast, the founder of the first Polish dynasty,

9

you not making mockery of me, speaking of Piast and the beginning now when I look for death, and have seen only misery in my life ? Have ye come to terrify me, crying : Darkness is coming ? Why would you terrify one who suffers ? Is not the terror of the grave enough ? Depart ! and tell God that if the sacrifice of my soul is accepted I will give it, and will agree that she shall die. My heart is so sorrowful that the angelic lights of the future world are abhorrent to me, and I am indifferent as to Eternity, and I would fain sleep.'

"And the angels interrupted him, saying : ' Thou dost ruin thyself. The desire of a man is his judgment upon him. And knowest thou not that perchance some life, yea, perchance the life and the fate of millions may depend on thy calm ? ' And Anhelli humbled himself and said : ' Angels, forgive me ! I will suffer as of old. My native language and human speech shall be silent within me as a harp with torn strings. To whom shall I speak ? Darkness shall be my companion and my country. But the horrors of the earth are nought, my anguish for my country is a greater horror. Why have I struggled and suffered torment for a thing that was madness ? Why did I not live at rest ? I cast myself into a river of woe, and its waves have carried me far, and now I shall return no more.'

" And again the angels interrupted him, saying : ' Thou didst blaspheme against thine own soul, and now thou blasphemest against the will which was in thee when thou didst consecrate thyself to thy country. Therefore we warn thee from the

Will of God that within a few hours thou shalt die : so be of more tranquil heart.'

" Hearing this, Anhelli bowed his head, and submitted to the Divine Will. And the angels departed. And when he remained alone, Anhelli cried out with a sorrowful voice : ' This, then, is already the end ! What have I done on earth ? Was it a dream ? '

" And while Anhelli pondered upon the hidden things of the future, the sky reddened and the glorious sun burst forth ; and, halting on the horizon, it arose no further, crimson as fire. Then the birds of the air and the white mews, which God had bidden flee before the darkness, availed them of the short day, and flew in great crowds, wailing. Then Anhelli looked on them, and said : ' Whither do you fly ? ' And it seemed to him that in the plaint of the birds he heard a voice answering him : ' We are flying to thy native land. Dost thou bid us greet anyone there ? Or, as we sit on some roof dear to thee, shall we sing in the night the song of sorrow, so that thy mother shall wake, or one of thy kin, and weep in the darkness for fear, thinking of the son whom the land of the grave hath swallowed, and the brother whom sorrow hath consumed ? '

" Such was the voice of the birds ; and Anhelli's heart broke within him, and he fell. And the sun sank under the earth, and there were only the birds flying ever higher, shining on the sapphire sky like wreaths of white roses, flying to the south.

" Anhelli was dead.

" In the darkness that then befell, there shone a great dawn from the south, and a fire of clouds.

And the tired moon sank into the flame of the skies, like a white dove falling at eventide on a hut red with the setting of the sun.

"Eloe sat by the body of the dead Anhelli. And lo! on a sudden a knight on a horse, all in armour, came forth from the fiery dawn, and he fled with a terrible rattle of hoofs. The snow ran before him and before the breast of the horse, like the foam of the waves before a boat. And in the hand of the knight was a banner, and on it burned three letters of fire.* And the knight reached in his flight Anhelli's dead body, and he cried out with a voice of thunder : ' Here is one who was a soldier. Let him rise! Let him mount on my horse, and I will carry him swifter than the storm. Lo, the nations are rising from the dead ! Lo, the streets of cities are paved with dead bodies ! He who hath a soul let him arise, let him live, for it is the hour for strong men to live.'

"Thus spoke the knight ; and Eloe, rising from the dead body, said : ' Knight, wake him not, for he sleeps. He was predestined to sacrifice, even the sacrifice of his heart. Knight, ride on, wake him not. This body belongs to me, and this heart was mine. Knight, thy horse stamps on his hoofs. Ride on ! '

"And the fiery knight fled away with the sound of a mighty storm ; and Eloe sat near Anhelli's dead body. And she was glad that his heart did not wake at the voice of the knight, and that he still slept."

So ends this strange and painful poem on that

* L U D, the Polish for Nation, People.

same deep note of melancholy that is the unrelieved setting of the whole work. He who has been the chosen victim for his nation may not even arise to behold her resurrection. In this figure of Anhelli, Krasinski sees the " generation which is languishing away in tears, in sorrow, in vain desires; and which will die on the day preceding the day in which those desires of theirs are to be fulfilled."*

* *Letters of Zygmunt Krasinski.* Vol. I. To Constantine Gaszynski, Nov. 18th, 1838.

CHAPTER VI

THE SPIRIT OF THE STEPPE

THE patriotic mysticism of Bohdan Zaleski, whom Mickiewicz termed the nightingale of Polish literature, takes a different tone to that of Messianism.

He was born in the Ukraine; the land whose immense, flower-strewn plains, sighing to the winds, inspire those who visit her as strangers with an intense melancholy, but those to whom she gives birth with an eternal nostalgia when parted from her. Zaleski, brought up in the steppes as a child, drew in the Ukrainian poetry and legends with the air he breathed. The Rising of 1830, in which he took part, drove him like so many others from his country : and he lived out half a century of exile in that incessant yearning for his native Ukraine that gives its wild and mournful music to his verse. He survived by thirty years his beloved friend, Adam Mickiewicz. Unlike the great trio of Polish poets who all died in their prime, he reached the extremity of bereaved and infirm old age. It was only in 1886 that he closed a singularly devout and pure life.*

Polish literature offers nothing quite similar to that one poem of Bohdan Zaleski's that stands distinct from all the rest of his work : the *Spirit of the Steppe* (1836). Obscure as it is, its beauty is

* S. Zdziarski, *Bohdan Zaleski*. Lwów (Polish).

mystical, ethereal, elusive. It is imbued with the magic and mystery of the steppes. The Ukraine lures her nursling back, as flesh of her flesh, after he has lost her for ever, to gaze on the successive pageants, sweeping over her plains and skies, of nations chosen by God and faithless to their calling. Then he beholds his own country, Poland, not in the triumph foretold to her by Messianism, but rather as one who has sinned, entering at last the everlasting gates.

A bald English rendering can but feebly reflect the exquisite opening of the poem. I only venture to offer it to the reader to whom the Polish language is not accessible by way of giving him some idea of its general drift.

> " And my mother, mother Ukraine,
>   And the mother, me, her son,
>   Cradled singing at her bosom.
>   Oh, the enchantress! in the aerial
>   Dawn, she saw the winged life
>   For her son, and, pitying, cried :
>   ' Nurse this child of mine, oh, Naiad !
>   With songs' milk and flowers' marrow
>   Nourish for flight this tender body.
>   Give him pictures in his dreams,
>   The centuries of my fair glory.
>   Let the folksongs of my people,
>   In hues of gold and hues of azure,
>   In a rainbow, flower about him.'
>
> " Sweet she was to me, oh, sweet !
>   No one, ever, anywhere,
>   Tenderer mother has caressed.

Those short years and days unknown,
Wrapped in miracle and secret,
Lie within my soul ensealed.
There my memory ever turneth,
Ever are my senses seeking
What has passed, a distant dream.

"Oh, the naiads of my mother,
With their kiss that rang in song,
Fired my blood for evermore.
To-day amid my country's torments,
Sad my heart and soul to death,
Still that blood forbids me sleep.

"And the mother, mother Ukraine,
When the star from heaven signalled,
Me, her son, her winged son,
Took she from the naiad's hand :
Stripped she off my down and feathers,
Bade my wings rise from the nest,
Tender omens and entreaties
Wailed she on her nestling's trail.

"'I the handmaid of the Lord,
Day by day my dearest children,
By the will of the earth's Father,
Send I as the snowdrift's plaything.
Now again my loved one flieth,
Knowing not as yet his cross.
Free his thought, and swift as wind,
To marvels clings and thirsts for song.
May he his life dream in the steppes,
The steppes, the world's destroyers' road.
There the wrath of God passed by.'"

She is seen no more, and only the enchantment of her memory remains to her son. " The moment eternally great and holy sweetens, with a breath of Paradise," his tears and sufferings under the cross. "Blessed be he who remembereth, somewhere in the years gone by, the sweet, strange, pure, and winged life, his first beginning. He who, in the torment of fleshly fetters, lifts his hands to heaven daily, yearneth to his ghostly memories."

These " ghostly memories " of the " winged life " on the steppes veil the whole poem with an atmosphere of mystery that enhances at once its romance and its charm. The mother of the poet's fancy has gone. But, ere he descends to the turmoil of life, he is caught up on his wings to the skies, " God's tent of molten gold." He is among the choirs who sing Hosanna before the throne. The angels are praying for him whose trial on earth is about to begin. He spreads his wings for the flight to the highest things ; but, for the first time, his thought knows bewilderment, and he returns " sad, to the abyss " of earth.

Then succeeds the poetical description of Bohdan's orphan boyhood and of his youth till the cry resounds from afar : " Poland, thy country ! " With tears, he, who " with each breath draws in the music of the steppe," says farewell to his family and to those same steppes. He is swept by the Rising into exile and into the tempest of the world. Poverty, temptation, sadness surround him. Toiling for his daily bread, he finds himself following in the secret of his thoughts the flight of the crane, living the life of the birds in the

free, untrammelled steppes. Ghosts of ages pass
dimly before him. He feels called to praise God
in a new song. An angelic voice summons him, as
with a blast of thunder, from on high : " Return,
oh, exile, to thy country." He wakes, weeping.
To which country, that on earth or the one in
heaven ? He returns to the land he loves ; but
not in the flesh, only in a vision.

Once more, then, his is the " winged life."

> " Breath of God, eternal breathing,
>   Wind of steppes, blowing light and dry,
>   Spreadeth as a couch beneath me,
>   Blows the down about my shoulders,
>   Swaddles me in its warm bosom."

It rocks him above the graves of those fallen in
the Ukraine, which was for centuries the scene of
border warfare in Polish history. He sees the
Black Sea, glittering as a counterfeit of the splen-
dours of dawn. " I see marvels, I hear marvels."
In a burst of light and music, the wizard-singer,
Bojan, the patriarchal poet of the Slav peoples,
sings to his golden- stringed zither his country's
welcome. Its sounds ring high and low over the
steppes, and the buried ages wake, till the fire and
the song alike fade into mist.

Floating on the wind, the poet then has a series
of visions, unrolling themselves over the steppes,
of the nations that have risen and fallen since the
beginning of the world. He begins with Eden and
the fall of man, reaches the Crucifixion, the
mission of the apostles, the ruin of Israel.

" Slept my spirit. I dreamed sweetly
    In a light, blest spirit dream.
    Shoreless time and time in space
    Shineth by the word of God,
    Singeth out the mighty epic.
    Million lights and million shadows,
    Worlds in flowers—the world's history—
    Blow in incense to the Lord."

He thus prefaces each stage of the chronicle
of the world that he passes in review. Hoofs
thunder in the steppes across which the hordes
sweep to the destruction of Rome. The wind
whispers mysterious messages to the forefathers
of his race. Rome falls, and the Rome of the
Papacy rises in her stead. The poet gives a rapid
summary of the centuries that follow, coloured
by his deep religious sense. Men sin repeatedly,
and the penalty ever descends afresh upon humanity. Then his spirit sleeps, and in his dream struggles
to escape as though to home. The voice of an
angel sighs in his ear : " The time of thy trial is
fulfilled. Behold this country, thine own land";
and with the eyes, not of the body:

" I see, I see a lovely land,
    Spaces stretching of broad meads,
    Mountains, forests, and two seas ;
    And a loved and mighty race,
    Sad and yearning, gaze through tears."

" Their great mother is in mourning. The
Poland of the Piasts, of the Jagiellos, once mistress

of Lithuania, Ruthenia, Silesia, has now no corner
of her soil free."

> " Silent everywhere our language,
>   Language in our hearts beloved.
>   As the instrument of angels,
>   Even so fair its melodies.
>   Must it then be whispered only ?
>   Hear, oh, Lord, our little children
>   Wailing from a hiding place.
>   Saddest fate ! they learn to fear
>   Their foe before they fear their God.

> ' And our women, weak and fainting,
>   For long years weep in the dust.
>   Their sons, their brothers, lie in graves,
>   Or wander at the world's far ends."

And the prophet-poets cry aloud with all their
strength the Polish songs : their voices are as
the wailing of the orphaned.

The singer is carried again on the wings of the
wind of the steppe, and swept to the Tatry—the
Carpathians—into the vision up to which the
whole poem has been leading. He sees on the summit
of the Polish mountains his mother Poland, but
a figure far removed from that under which
Mickiewicz and Krasinski delighted to symbolize
her. Here she is the beautiful repentant sinner.
" She has loved and she has wandered. She has
knelt for years in ashes." Her hair streams in
grief and penitence, dishevelled, to the wind.
Her cheek has faded for mourning. Beside her sit
her sisters who have shared her fate : Lithuania,

taking refuge in her bosom, the Ukraine, "beautiful, incarnate song," who weeps, and through her tears looks upon "me, her son." The procession of Poland's dead heroes gathers about her: and her sisters, kneeling, cry to heaven the word so beloved by Zaleski :

"Great her sins, but surely, Lord,
Greater still Thy mercy is."

Rainbows flash from heaven, and ever louder is the song of the angels and of the apostles of Slavonia : "Honour and glory to the Magdalen. We carry the absolution of the Lord. Raise the penitent's head. The Lord is arming the archangel. The time of the Holy Ghost draws nigh. The world shall gather strength in the grace of the cross. From the seed of repentant Poland the future generations shall flower in fruit to the Lord. The archangel himself at their head shall lead them to the last battle with evil." Amidst the hosannas of numberless multitudes of the saints, the poet beholds his nation arise from the dust of her repentance, her youth given back to her. "I see marvels, I hear marvels." In this supreme moment he returns to the mystic note of the Ukraine. The same light and music that flashed around the steppe when he returned there in spirit from his exile, now beat from the heavenly fires. Once more the voice of the wizard and the sound of his zither peal over the Ukraine. "Glory, honour ! She shall rise ! " is the song of Bojan. He stretches his instrument over all the countries of Slavonia ; and the sweet melody streams forth,

"The flock, the snow-white flock, is floating,
The wizard-singer's swan-like song
Sounds one long prophetic word
To the future, hope in song.
Still that word rings in my ear,
Ever dwells within my heart,
In my heart for ever fondled.

"Let our Poland rise for ever !
At the day of the great banquet,
In the choir I will, Slavonia,
Repeat to you the song of Bojan.
Suffering in one flash shall pass."

Again, on the " wind of the steppe, the breath
of God, his aerial couch," he is carried in the mists
that are gathering about him. Through the
whistle of the winds, he hears a sad, wild melody.
The third cock crows. Voices of the dead un-
baptized children who, in the Ukrainian legends,
wander through the snow and storm, crying for
baptism and Paradise, wail in the tempest. Like
them the poet, a son of earth, hungers too early
for the " angelic bread " he may not touch yet.
Like them, he is unable to enter heaven, for he is
fettered by the vesture of flesh. He returns to his
own place in a hard world. He sees no more the
vision, the memory of which wakes eternal sadness in his soul.

"Where that flight, that far, wide flight ?
Where heard I that mighty epic ?
Worlds in flowers, the world's history ?
Where that golden-stringed singer ? "

He has gazed on the miracles of the universe, and they cannot perish from his eyes or heart. Man may call what the poet saw a dream. "Are the tears of my life a dream? Poland, the Ukraine, a dream?" he asks, with the mingled passion of the patriot and the mystic who, in the body or out of the body, had beheld things unseen by mortal eyes. "Blessed be he who remembereth somewhere in the years gone by, the sweet, strange, pure, and winged life, his first beginning. He who, in the torment of fleshly fetters, lifts his hands to heaven daily, yearneth to his ghostly memories."

"According to Zaleski," said Mickiewicz in the Collège de France, "it is not the desire to sing the exploits of some celebrated chief, it is not the love of popularity, it is not the love of art that can form a poet. You must have been pre-destined, you must have been attached by mysterious bonds to the country that you are to sing one day: and to sing is nothing else than to reveal the thought of God, which rests on that country and on the people to which the poet belongs."*

* Adam Mickiewicz, *Les Slaves.*

CHAPTER VII

THE IDEALS OF KORNEL UJEJSKI

BY the year 1860, the great triad of Polish poets, Mickiewicz, Krasinski, and Slowacki, had passed from the world. But, in a certain measure, their mantle may be said to have fallen upon a poet of the succeeding generation, whose poetry has appealed so strongly to the hearts of his countrymen that his famous *Chorale* has passed into the treasury of Polish national songs. Kornel Ujejski—born in 1823, dead in 1897—can scarcely, in point of birth, be considered as belonging to a younger generation than Zygmunt Krasinski, who was only eleven years his senior; but he survived him by nearly forty years, wrote under different conditions, and had been, moreover, a mere child during those disasters of the thirties that changed the lives of Mickiewicz, Krasinski, and Slowacki. Thus his work, from a literary and moral standpoint, reads as that of one who came later.

He was the son of a noble house in Austrian Poland. The poet's private life, with the exception of the year of massacre in 1846, was outwardly prosperous, and experienced none of the afflictions which fell to the lot of Mickiewicz and Krasinski. And yet over the greater part of his poetry, and especially over its finest portion, hangs a not less, perhaps even deeper, sadness than that stamped on the writings of his predecessors. So terrible was the ordeal through which every devout son of Poland passed in the early years of her mourning, the thirties of the nineteenth century, that an inheritance of profound melancholy was the inevitable birthright even of those Polish poets who were only children at the time. The Polish child was of necessity not only brought up on a chronicle of sorrow, but those sorrows were living, were present to him. Dismembered Poland was harassed by oppression. Ujejski said of himself that from his early childhood an atmosphere of tragedy enveloped him ; that his first impressions of the world were such as to banish from his heart all childish joy, and to make his poetry a song of grief.* " Bitter is the condition of the Pole in every part of the wide earth," wrote Krasinski. This of itself alone would suffice to explain the general tone of Ujejski's work ; and when we remember that, after he had reached manhood, he beheld the calamities of 1846 and of the sixties overwhelm his nation, it is little wonder that his poems are among the saddest in Polish literature.

Like the other great poets of his race, Ujejski's poetical ideal, early conceived and put into practice equally early, was that of a moral and national teacher. We have seen how Poland looked to her poets for help and guidance. Ujejski, then, chose his calling, and remained faithful to it all his life. His prayer was, so he sings in his poem on the death of Mickiewicz, to follow in the latter's footsteps, and speak to his people of the same national faith that Mickiewicz taught, albeit he

* A. Mazanowski, *Kornel Ujejski* (Polish).

confesses he cannot do so with a power like to that of the greater poet ; to use the Polish lyre, however heavy the burden to himself, as an instrument of blessing, and never of evil, to his nation.

His love for his country soon found its way into verse. In one of his first poems—*The Song of the Grain* (1843)—the never-dying hopes of nature can teach him and his nation, for all their weary hearts, the moral of a new life to be born again. The sun sets, and with it the symbol of liberty. But the stars rising remind him that there are other stars, the stars, that is, of the faith and homely virtue of the peasants tilling the fields, that shall be as guiding fires to all Poland.

" And our grief grows lighter, our hearts ache less, knowing that the flame trembles in every little spark," and that great luminaries may be fashioned in time out of united stars.

Then, going out into the meadows at daybreak to sow the grain, when " all the air is singing like a lark," he learns the lesson of the wheat. The reader will remember how in Frank Norris' noble novel *The Octopus : The Epic of the Wheat*, after long anguish Vanamee, wandering through the night, sees the dawn flaming over ranchos once bare, now white with wheat, and reads therein that life springs from death, immortality from corruption, joy from pain, even as the seed fructifies out of dark places. To the young Pole, writing half a century earlier, the wheat speaks in like manner and, as he watches the peasants sowing the grain, he consoles himself in his heavy sorrow by the thought that the sons will reap where the fathers sowed. The sower will pass to the grave with the words on his lips :

" 'I die, but the seed will not die.' Oh, it were sweet to dream thus in the hour preceding death ! "

And another will take his place who can sow in his turn, and who will not spare his toil. Storms may beat upon the furrows ; but Mother Earth shields the seed in her bosom, and slowly the spirit breathes and gives it life. And at last the poet beholds the fields golden with the harvest while the reapers load the waggons, singing songs of joy and freedom.

A year after he had written this poem, Ujejski saw Warsaw for the first time. This visit to the capital of his country, then groaning beneath the heel of Nicholas I., had a far reaching influence on the young poet's subsequent life as a writer. Not only did it lay the foundations of the poem *Marathon* by which he made his name, but it was in Warsaw, with the spectacle of the nation's suffering before him, that he was inspired with the clear comprehension of his particular vocation. He tells us in the poem *The Lyre of Jeremias*, which he wrote in Warsaw, that now he casts his old lyre underfoot :

" For I can sing no longer for myself. I stretch my hand to Jeremias' lyre to string it to the wailing of my brothers. I renounce myself. I cast all my own sorrows to the bottom of my heart ; let them perish without echo. My whole nation is my family. Mine are the tears from her eyes, mine the blood from her wounds. Suffering her pain, I will sing. Ah, I suffer ! "

He sits sorrowing and alone, with a city in mourning about him. His friends are gone, slain, or in the living graves of Siberia ; and, as he watches at night,

" I hear the subterranean hollow drag of chains. I hear far off the beating of the hammer. It is my brothers toiling in the mines."

He sees his people in the snowy deserts, perishing of hunger and cold, dying with no memory left of them. And, likening the tears of Poland to those of Jerusalem, the poet, falling on his face for grief, cries upon the spirit of Jeremias, his favourite type of a national inspirer and prophet, to give him of his strength, for he sinks beneath his sorrow.

We shall see later with what deep psychological significance this figure of Jeremias is invested in Ujejski's eyes.

Up to the year of Ujejski's visit to Warsaw, his name was scarcely known. Then, after his return to Austrian Poland, as he was taking part one evening in a literary gathering in a friend's house, the boy of twenty-two read aloud a poem that he had just finished writing, entitled *Marathon*. Such was the patriotic power, the finished artistic beauty, of these lines that the audience sat spellbound in silent wonder and admiration. From that hour, Ujejski took his place among the great poets of his nation.

His purpose in writing *Marathon* may be gathered from the words of stinging reproach to his countrymen which form the preface, and from the quotation out of Byron which he chooses as his motto :

" The mountains look on Marathon,
   And Marathon looks on the sea ;
And musing there an hour alone,
   I dream'd that Greece might still be free,
For standing on the Persian's grave,
I could not deem myself a slave."

" You ask a song," so Ujejski flings his poem forth into the world, " of charm and sweetness for your ears ; but, my compatriots, my only song for you is one that shall remind you of the clanking of your chains. You ask a song as a flower in a garland to give you honour at the banquet ; but I would fain steel your enervated souls in a blush of fire like armour in the flame."

Then he laments that to him, a youth, has fallen the task of spreading this language of sarcasm and upbraiding instead of that of love. He has long sought for some means by which he can infuse manhood into the hearts of men who are growing weak in bondage ; and now he will raise the heroes of ancient history to point the way.

And so he sings the story of Marathon ; in other words, of the victory of a few routing, by the strength of one common bond of devotion to their fatherland, the hosts of Persia. The poem opens with the burning of Sardis.

" A slave ran out from the burning town, and behind him ran in pursuit the wails of the dying that rang in his ears. And he fled, veiled by the darkness of night. Oft he cast backward his terrified eyes, and behind him the wind breathed fire on the heights, and carried clamour upon it. He stood and he listened. Perchance even now the enemies butcher his brothers, give the aged mother to drink of the blood of her son, and level the hut with fire and with sword. But tarry he may not. With the satrap's command, oh, runner, speed on, for the way is still long. When thou returnest thou shalt count the corpses in ashes. He fled through the desert with the news he was bearing, and swiftly he ran till the sun had arisen; and when at the outposts he met with a runner, 'Sardis is in flames. To Susa! To Susa!' he cried, and he turned; and the other, like an ostrich wide spreading its wings, flew, and vanished before the sun like a spectre of night."

In a series of virile word-paintings, Ujejski tersely but vigorously depicts the march to war of the Persian armies, the terror in Athens, the victory.

"From the four ends of the world the legions march. From the four ends of the world the vultures flock; until a mighty wind springs up from the fluttering of the flags, and a mighty humming from the rattling of the bows. The earth is blackened with the horses' hoofs."

Meanwhile, in Athens we have the moral point of the poem, that is, the speech of Miltiades, bidding him who would prefer to be a slave begone to Darius and to fawn upon him, like a hungry cur, for empty honours.

"But we others, let us remain, we who are linked in misfortune. Either we will wipe out the foe with this sword, or, by the holy gods, will we, free, find refuge from slavery in death."

Impressing upon the Athenian crowds that,

united, they are all-powerful against the most
overwhelming odds, he reminds them that their
ancestors are summoning them to the like glorious
deeds as theirs.

Ujejski hardly describes the battle itself except
to insist again upon that dominant, and to the
Pole most significant, note of a handful confounding a multitude. The action transfers itself to
Athens, to the women and old men awaiting
tidings till the night is broken by the sound of
hurrying feet, and the messenger, crying victory
through the streets, falls dead without a wound.

" On the battle-field after the murderous day-
long game is played, after the bloody toil, the
raging war, thousands of men sleep now in peace.
The Greek and Persian on one self-same bed lie
without anger in eternal brotherhood. Over them
ravens stalk and feast, and with hoarse voices bid
their brethren to the banquet come."

Marathon was written in 1845. The following
year Poland was stricken by one of the most terrible
tragedies that she has ever known, the uprising
of the Galician peasantry against the Polish nobles.
Their ignorance exploited by secret agents,
driven on by the instigations of the Austrian
government, the peasants fell upon their land-
lords' houses and put the inhabitants to tortures,
butchering men, women, and children. Whole
families perished together at their hands. Terror
reigned over the land.

Belonging as he did to a noble house, Ujejski,
although he himself and his immediate family
escaped destruction, lived in the midst of these
scenes. The grief and horror of his soul are stamped

upon the poems that streamed forth from his pen at this time. Passionately patriotic, devoted to the purest of national ideals, he saw the nation that he loved thrust down into a pit of abasement, dragged from the path of glory and salvation which he and every poet of his race had looked to see her tread, her fair fields become a shambles. For once his heart seems to fail him, and he complains that he can see God no longer. Nature, that had inspired him with the hope of the wheat, is now only cruel, parading her beauty, indifferent to human anguish.

"Oh, Earth, there is no heart nor love in thee. As a coquette decking herself at evening, thou dreamest only of ornaments, of splendour. Thou art an egotist. Drowned in thy flowers, thou dost forget thy suffering children. Gladly thou catchest every different voice, except one only— except the voice of pain.

"Many a time thy treacherous hand has woven from the thorns thou bearest a crown of torment for thy child. That guilty thorn, drunken with innocent blood, blooms again as a white flower in the spring, and the birds sing of it to the world : 'Oh, what a white and stainless flower ! '

"And over our flaming homes, when the conflagrations fling wide their crimson flags, and the mother, with her hair sparkling in the glare, casts herself on the cradle of her child ; then the cloud floating in the dark night skies thus whispers to itself : 'See the gay fires that flame upon the earth. Oh, but they paint my bosom with their beauty ! '

"Oh, Earth, thou ever, ever art the same. A

demon of irony flies always over thee that makes
our pain thine ornament, thy splendour. They
say that amber is a bird's tear, turned to stone.
Oh, Earth, our blood is but a ruby to thee, our
cry of grief thy music, our whitened bones thy
easy couch.

" To-day I saw a string of cranes fly from across
the sea, lured by the spring. And they flew fast,
and with a joyful song they hailed the pond where
lilies float, and hailed the hills with pine-trees
crowned, and the silver rivers on the carpeted
meads. And, flying their free trail above this
earth, nought, nought they saw or heard—except
the spring. I wept, and in my heart I said : ' Oh,
Lord, why am I not a bird ? ' Old wish ! Age
after age repeats, better to be a bird than be a
man " (*The Earth*, 1846).

Under the burden of his own distress of mind
and of his country's agony, Ujejski, like the other
Polish poets who had gone before him, poured
out his soul in poetical inspiration. The figure of
Jeremias, lamenting among the ruins of a fallen
city, had already, as we have seen, captivated his
imagination. In the midst of the fresh national
disaster, he now turned again in thought to another
oppressed race who had wept by the waters of
strange lands—to the Hebrews of old. The peculiar part that their prophet-poets had played in
raising and inspiring them spoke straight to
Ujejski's heart. His nation was now the outcast
of peoples. He would send her a message of counsel
and of consolation under the impersonation of a
second Jeremias. Thus arose that famous cycle
of lyrics that are among the most mournful poems

even of Poland's tragic literature—Ujejski's *Complaints of Jeremias*.

Jeremias, the type of a national guide, flies, an angel of vengeance, over Poland. The land is one lake of blood. The skies are red with the fires of burning homes. The wails of the dying are mingled with the hoarse cries of the murderers. And Jeremias calls upon the nation to retaliate, and avenge her wrongs by bloodshed on her side. She has been patient long enough. Heaven will not take pity on the weak, but gives the victory to brute strength.

" ' Oh, Lord, Thou, Who weighest in Thy hand our fate, open Thy heavens to this song. And when that day of ours shall come, that yearned-for day, bid Thy angels thunder on brazen trumpets to the four quarters of the world this watchword in that day : Revenge ! Revenge ! Revenge ! '

" And the nation trembled and moved : but, dragged down by her chain, she fell once more, for she breathed not the spirit of God, and it was not in God but revenge, that she woke from sleep."

Then Jeremias repents him of his evil bidding till at last, after long penance, his tongue is loosened to sing a higher strain of prayer and praise.

" Oh, my people ! " cries the poet, in conclusion to this, his preliminary poem, *The Word of Jeremias :* " These songs of mine are my life's blood. Let this one word ring in your inspirations, let it flow in your veins. Let it die not on your lips before the jeering foe, and you shall need no other pillory for the foe—sorest punishment for Satan—than this word, *Praised be God.*"

The moral teaching of this poem is the more striking, when we realise not only that it came from the heart of a youth at an age when the blood runs hottest at the sight of wrong, but that he was not, as it were, merely writing on paper, far removed from the passion of the conflict. What he described was a matter that touched his own life to the quick. The deep religious feeling and high ideal with which these lines are impregnated are the key-note of Ujejski's life-work.

The succeeding poems of the series continue on the like tone of faith, of pain, of prayer under intolerable affliction. As the poet keeps vigil on a summer's night, his soul revolts against the beauty and tranquillity of that night, where no trace remains of the tears that have watered it, of the blood with which it has streamed. The leaves are motionless on the trees, and swans dream where the lakes reflect the stars.

" The earth smells sweet, and the dawn flames. My God ! My God ! " is his horror-stricken refrain.

At another moment, he will paraphrase the Our Father, turning each of its invocations into a heart-broken entreaty for his nation.

" Oh, let the nations troubled by eternal war breathe again in brotherhood and peace. Let this earth be engirdled by liberty and love. Let there be one God, one aim, one race. *Thy Kingdom come.*

" Oh, then, then it were worth while to live, in liberty beneath Thy care. To-day we knock in vain against the coffin's lid. *Thy Will be done.*"

In the *Chorale*, which Ujejski wrote before the

other poems of the cycle and to which he subsequently added the latter, he reaches the height of power as a national and a moral poet, calling to the deepest things of the heart. One of the finest poems that he ever composed, it is still sung in Poland and at Polish gatherings, and remains among the best loved poems of his country.

"With the smoke of the burning fires, with the dust soaked with our brothers' blood, this voice oh, Lord, beats up to Thee. Terrible is this our complaint. This is the last sigh of ours. Our hair grows white from such prayers as these. We know no songs now without complaint. The crown of thorns has grown into our brows. Eternally, as a monument to Thine anger, our imploring hands are stretched out to Thee.

"How many times hast Thou not scourged us! And we, not yet cleansed from our fresh bleeding wounds, we cry out again : ' He has heard us and pardoned, for He is our Father, for He is our Lord.' And we rise again more firmly hoping, and again by Thy will our enemy crushes us ; and he flings us his gibe like a rock on our bosoms : ' *Now where is that Father and where is that God ?* '

"And we look to the sky to see if a hundred suns will not fall from its height, as a sign to our foes. All is still, all is still. In the blue the free bird still soars as of old. Then, rent asunder by fearful doubt, ere we can waken again our faith, our lips blaspheme Thee, though our hearts are weeping. Oh, judge us by our hearts, not by our words.

"Oh, Lord, Lord, to the horror of the world

time has brought on us a terrible story. The son
has slain his mother, the brother has slain his
brother : a multitude of Cains is among us now.
Lord, it is not they who are guilty, though they
have thrust back our future ; but other demons
have done this deed. Oh, punish the hand, not
the blind sword.

" See, in our misery ever the same, to Thy
breast, to Thy stars we float on prayer, like birds
fain to sleep flying to rest in the nests that are
theirs. Shelter us, shelter us with the hand of a
father. Give us the vision of Thy mercies to come.
Let the flower of martyrdom lull us by its fragrance, let the light of martyrdom surround us
with glory.

" And with Thy archangel to lead us we will
then go on to the mighty battle, and Satan's
cowering body transfix with Thy conquering
banner. We will open our hearts to our erring
brothers ;* the oil of freedom shall cleanse their
guilt. And then shall the abject blasphemer hearken to our answer : ' *God was and God is.*' "
(*Chorale*, 1846).

All through Ujejski's poetry, and most notice-
ably in the *Complaints of Jeremias*, written though
they were under such tragic circumstances, the
poet's attitude is never pessimistic.† Even in the

---

* Were it only from his expressions in the *Chorale* we should
learn how completely Ujejski had pardoned the Galician peasantry ;
but his whole life, spent in working in their behalf, speaks for itself.

† It may be said that *The Earth* and a fragment which he wrote
at the same time, during the massacres, and in which he says,
" Terror blanched my face, I saw not God," convey an impression
of utter hopelessness. But such language is so unusual with Ujejski
that it must be considered as exceptional, and only representing a
moment of agony, not the habit of his mind.

hours of his deepest desolation, his confidence in a Divine ordering, however terrible the test by which it is tried, does not falter. The ideals that he places before the eyes of the youth of Poland are invariably those of faith, moral purity, constancy, and hope. His grief, indeed, seems to approach despair in that poem from the *Complaints of Jeremias* where, at the end of each of the eight stanzas in which the poet commemorates the sufferings of his country, tolls the cry of pain : " Oh, God, we are sorrowful." The nation, he says, has drunk to the dregs of her chalice. Upon the burning pyres of our brethren, on our sons thirsting at the stakes, heaven casts not dew, but thunderbolts. " We are filled with tears and mourning " that our homes know us no more but are given over to the stranger, while our bones are scattered over the wide world. The swallows chirp in their own tongue, but the Polish child no longer hears his language. Birds of passage may return, with the spring, to their country ; the Pole, driven to the snows of Siberia, may never return again, and only the dead bodies of those fallen by the wayside mark his road.

" Then, Lord, wilt Thou never console Thy repentant people ? We wither as leaves before Thine eyes ; and wilt Thou not hasten the hour of redemption ? "

But even here the poet can still reiterate that his nation kneels before her God. Ujejski, in fact, is always and definitely on the side of the angels. The *Act of Faith* that closes the *Complaints* shows us an undismayed soul that rose victorious above the temptations that encompass the children of a suffering and persecuted nation.

" Long I wept in the garden of Gethsemane. Long I tore the music of my lyre out from my tears. Now I rise me with a wearied body, but with a strong, a mighty and anointed soul."

Poland, having lain in the dust of humiliation, soars upward, crowned with stars. Ujejski dictates to her her act of faith. Here he follows more closely in the steps of Krasinski than in any other of his poems. The echoes of the great Messianistic prophecies that reached their noblest confession in Krasinski's *Psalm of Good Will* cling about the lips of the younger poet likewise. Ujejski's poetry is never so decided an expression of the theories of Messianism as we find in Mickiewicz's *Ancestors* and Krasinski's *Dawn* and *Psalms of the Future*. He is, indeed, far more what we might call Western in his line of thought, more concrete. But this *Act of Faith* is a clear testimony to Messianistic hopes.

" We believe, Lord, oh, firmly we believe that Thou hast sent us as a torch by night to lead the human race to Thee. We believe that the light of our dawn is already dawning in the skies. We believe that Thou sowest stars upon our road. We believe that though Thou dost permit at times the weak to stagger, yet Thou dost shield us all from fall, and that Thou hast set Thy angels round the pit. We believe, oh, Lord, we are the sons of light. We believe that, in some time not far away, our country's bounds shall be from sea to sea, and all the nations will through the ages and the ages gaze on us, as man gazes to the sun. We believe, oh, Lord, that Thou shalt rule us as our King."

The *Complaints of Jeremias* touch the highest point of Ujejski's national aspirations, and created a profound impression in his country. Under the literary aspect, he showed himself here as a master of lyrical form, whose love of music gave his poetry a peculiar rhythmic charm. The patriotic fire that trembles through these poems never died. Using again the image of the chosen race, in which so many of the Polish poets saw the mystic counterpart of their own people, Ujejski wrote his *Biblical Melodies*. Albeit the subjects are scriptural, reading between the lines and especially in *Super Flumina Babylonis*, we know that the Polish singer is in reality writing of no nation of the past, but of his Poland under a veil, letting these lessons of fidelity to a national cause, steadfastness under oppression, hope in the future, speak for themselves.

But it would be a mistake to imagine that the nature of Ujejski's patriotism is purely one of resignation and passive endurance. There is a strong martial side to it. The *Angelus*, peaceful evening picture though it is, has yet a sterner and a rugged colouring. The mists of the coming night droop about the hamlet. Homing birds fly, crying, to their nests. The peasant boy in the hills is piping on his flute. Then the Angelus rings out from the village church. The scent of the flowers, the mist, the murmuring of the stream, the clamour of the birds, the flute of the boy, all join their voices in song and prayer. The sound of the bell reaches the dead in their graves who died for Poland, and they, too, pray. Then the poet asks of fate that when he, in his turn, goes down into his grave, after having sung to its depths the sorrow of his nation, with his last tears given to the mother earth he loved so well, these same evening sounds may breathe over him, as his dying lips repeat the Angelus.

" Let them lay me in my coffin on a bloody shield. Let my songs of war murmur there around me. Let me dream that, dying, I beheld an armed people, radiant in their victory."

Many years later, he prays that when he has finished his work of song for his nation :

" May that beloved earth, that natal earth, fall on my bosom as though she mourned for me. She will not lie heavily on me who loved her. Softly as a mother's hand, will she rest upon mine eyes."

And he bids that his bones shall be laid in a meadow that he knows, where, so popular tradition has it, the sons of Poland fell in the past fighting for their country, and where a legend foretells that the final victory of Poland will be fought. There, says the poet, spring blooms earlier, the winds blow more freshly and more sweetly than in any other spot. There, the ghosts of those who gave up their lives for Poland hold nightly procession.

" Bear me there. Lay my head there beneath the turf. Let that great hope be my glory. I reck not whether they bury me with lamenting and with weeping ; but let that mighty hope be my death monument."

" Oh, earth of my songs," cries the poet with all the passion of the Pole for the soil. " Oh, thou

Q

who art my mother! Thou, who dost lavish comfort on thy faithful sons, thou wilt not drive my yearning soul away from thee."

There he will lie till above his head resounds the clash of arms, and the peasants rise for Poland, the nation battles for her freedom. In that day of triumph, of a conflict such as the world has never yet seen, in that day " I will arise again."

The pastoral scenes that he has painted in the *Ang lus* were the setting of most of Ujejski's life. He married in 1849, and, as he sings in a poem to his wife, found in his happy marriage a refuge from adversity. From that time he spent nearly all of his tranquil days in the country, surrounded by domestic joys, devoting himself to unwearied labour for the welfare of the Galician peasants. From his youth upwards their condition had always been a subject dear to his heart. Their poverty and misfortunes are the theme of more than one of his poems, written to awake sympathy for their lot. For the last seventeen years of his life he wrote little. But his nation was never forgotten. Not long before his death, on the celebration of his poetical jubilee, he said that life had deceived him, for it had given him what he had neither sought nor wished, fame and honours, but it had withheld from him the one desire of his heart, the resurrection of Poland. His place in Polish literature is that of a great lyric poet, and of a teacher who never ceased to urge the youth of his nation towards the highest ideals, personal and national, and to inspire them with an evergreen hope for the restoration of their beloved and oppressed nation. These two tenets

of hope and resurrection were his own cherished
and life-long beacon-lights. We may, indeed,
look upon them as being his last testament, the
last words by which he chose to be remembered.
For it was he who raised the inscription over the
gate of the country graveyard near his home,
where his dust was to lie : " They shall rest and
they shall rise."

TABLE OF VARIOUS DATES IN POLISH HISTORY

600. Birth of Cracow.

842. Foundation of the Piast dynasty, the earliest line of Polish sovereigns.

963. Conversion to Christianity of Mieczyslaw I., which brings about the conversion of Poland.

992-1025. Reign of Boleslaw I. He unites Poland, is victorious over Bohemia, Germany, and Russia, and establishes the archbishopric of Gnesen.

1079. Murder by Boleslaw II. of St. Stanislas, Bishop of Cracow.

1139. Poland is divided into duchies.

1177-1194. Reign of Casimir II., the Just, who reunites Poland, and founds the nucleus of the Polish senate.

1194. Poland again divided into duchies.

1226. Rise of the Teutonic Knights in Polish history. Summoned by Conrad, Duke of Masovia, to assist him against Prussia, they become the deadliest enemies of Poland and the founders of modern Prussia.

1241. First of the Tartar invasions that ravage Poland for centuries and against which she stands as the bulwark of Christendom.

1295. Poland is again a kingdom.

1331. First general Diet.

1333. Accession of Casimir III., the Great, whose reign ushers in the golden period of Polish history, and confers peace and prosperity on the nation.

1335. Silesia ceded to Bohemia.*

1340. Lwów and Red Ruthenia (Eastern Galicia) united to the Polish crown.

1343. Pomerania with Danzig ceded to the Teutonic Knights.

1347. Statute of Wiślica which codifies Polish laws.

1352. Volhynia annexed by Poland.

1364. Foundation of the University of Cracow.

1370. Extinction of the Piast dynasty with the death of Casimir III.

1386. The marriage of Jadwiga, Queen of Poland, with Jagiello, Prince of Lithuania, unites Lithuania and Ruthenia to Poland, which latter consequently becomes the greatest state in Eastern Europe. The Jagiello dynasty is thus founded.

1410. Victory over the Teutonic Knights at Grünwald which has remained one of the favourite episodes of Polish history.

1466. Peace of Thorn between Poland and the Teutonic Knights. Western Prussia with Danzig revert to Poland, the Teutonic Knights retaining Eastern Prussia as a fief under the Polish King.

1473. Birth of Copernicus.

1525. Albert of Brandenburg, Grand Master of

---

* With the exception of two of its duchies that the Poles regained in the fifteenth century, Silesia never returned to Poland. But to this day a large Polish population is to be found in Silesia who have remained faithful to their language and their origin.

the Teutonic Knights, having embraced Lutheranism, retains Eastern Prussia as a secular and hereditary state held under the Polish crown.

1561. Livonia passes to Poland.

1572. Death of Sigismund II. Augustus closes the Jagiello line, and from being nominally, the Polish crown becomes practically, elective.

1574. The Pacta Conventa are drawn up by which the rule of the state passes from the hands of the king to those of the nation.

1576-1586. Reign of Stephen Batory strengthens Poland. He organizes the Cossacks as a defence to the Polish frontiers, and is victorious over Russia and the Turks.

1587. Opening of the Vasa dynasty with the accession of Sigismund III., in whose reign Warsaw becomes the capital and wars are waged with Sweden, Russia, Tartars, and Turks.

1595. Union of Brześć, which unites the Greek Church of Ruthenia to that of Rome, and is the origin of the Ruthenian Uniates.

1621. Victory under Chodkiewicz over Turks and Tartars at Chocim.

1648. Beginning of the Cossack revolt against Poland.

1648. The disastrous reign of John Casimir begins during which Poland fights Tartars, Cossacks, Sweden, Russia, and Prussia.

1652. First exercise of the *liberum veto* by which at the word of a single deputy the Polish Diet could be dissolved.

1655. Repulse of the Swedes at Czenstochowa by the prior Kordecki, which saves the whole of Poland.

1660. Treaty of Oliwa, by which Poland yields most of Livonia to Sweden, and Prussia formally renounces allegiance to Poland.

1667. Treaty of Andruszowo, by which Smolensk, Kiev and the left bank of the Dnieper pass to Russia, and Poland loses her suzerainty over the Cossacks.

1673. Victory under John Sobieski over the Turks at Chocim.

1674. Accession of John Sobieski.

1683. Sobieski delivers Vienna and the whole of Christendom from the Turks.

1697-1763. Decay of Poland under the rule of the Electors of Saxony.

1763. With the death of Augustus III. the struggle for Poland's existence against Russia, Prussia, and Austria enters its acute stage.

1764. Accession of Stanislas Poniatowski, last King of Poland.

1768-1772. Confederation of Bar, led by the Pulawskis, fights against Russia in defence of the national liberty and religion.

1772. First partition of Poland between Russia, Prussia, and Austria.

1788-1791. The Four Years' Diet, held in what remained of independent Poland.

1791. On the third of May the Polish Diet passes the Liberal Constitution of Poland.

1793. Second partition of Poland between Russia and Prussia.

1794.   Rising led by Kościuszko for the national independence.

1794.   Defeat at Maciejowice, at which Kościuszko is taken prisoner, massacre of Praga, and capture of Warsaw by Suvorov.

1795.   Third partition of Poland between Russia, Prussia, and Austria.

1798.   Birth of Adam Mickiewicz.

1807.   Treaty of Tilsit, by which Napoleon creates the Duchy of Warsaw.

1815.   Treaty of Vienna, by which Poland is re-divided between Austria, Russia, and Prussia ; autonomous Kingdom of Poland under Russia guaranteed ; and the Free Republic of Cracow established.

1830.   The first Polish Rising.

1831.   Warsaw is taken by the Russians and the Rising ends.

1846.   The Galician massacres.

1846.   Annexation of Cracow by Austria.

1855.   Death of Adam Mickiewicz.

1861.   Species of autonomy granted to Austrian
1863-64.   The second Polish Rising.   [Poland.

1871.   Opening of the Kulturkampf by Bismarck, and persecution of the national Church in Prussian Poland.

1885.   Expulsion by Bismarck of forty thousand Poles from Prussian Poland.

1886.   The Colonisation Bill passed by the Prussian Diet for the purchase and Germanization of Polish land.

1908.   Expropriation Bill passed by which the Polish landowner in Prussian Poland is forcibly evicted.

PRESS NOTICES OF
" ADAM MICKIEWICZ, THE NATIONAL POET OF POLAND "

" Miss Gardner, a devoted and accomplished student of Polish literature, has performed a considerable service in making better known the life and work of the most famous of Polish poets. His pathetic story is told . . . with deep sympathy by Miss Gardner. . . . Some of her prose renderings are of great beauty—often with the wild and wayward beauty which we associate with Chopin."
—*Manchester Guardian.*

" Miss Gardner gives us a remarkably true picture of the relations between the poet and his country. . . . Miss Gardner has realized fully what she attempted, and indeed few countrymen of the poet could perform the task better."—*Cambridge Review.*

" The work is so admirably done that it would be welcome, though we had other biographies or other critical appreciations of the Polish poet. This remarkable work. . . ."—*Tablet.*

" This is the first attempt which has been made in our language to capture the imagination by a critical study of the fine character and high achievements of Adam Mickiewicz. Miss Monica Gardner writes exceedingly well—with knowledge, with sympathy, and with vision."—*Standard.*

" Her sympathies with that oppressed nationality, a sinister monument of the triumph of might over right, and her understanding of the Polish spirit, make her pages inspiring reading. Her work will do much to make the fame of a great poet, already well enough known on the continent, spread into England."—*Month*.

" One would have been grateful for a moderate biography of Poland's national poet. Miss Gardner's work merits a more distinguished adjective, and therefore is doubly worthy of attention. . . She explains his masterpieces with sympathy and skill, giving at the same time workmanlike translations of the more famous passages."—*Athenæum*.

" Miss Gardner has not given us a literary book alone, but the story of a soul, and of a soul which mirrored in itself the travail and agony of a nation. . . . This vivid and sympathetic record . . . . Miss Gardner has done no small service in making his rare nature and gifts known to the English world."—*Dublin Review*.

" His life Miss Gardner has admirably described. She is to be congratulated on the courage and perseverance which have produced such a good book on a subject which has been too long neglected."—*Times*.

" C'est, à notre connaissance, le premier livre anglais qui traite avec tant d'ampleur et tant de conscience une question d'histoire littéraire polonaise. . . . Ce brillant coup d'essai."—
Bulletin Polonais.

INDEX